"This is a giant leap of recognition by Whittemore, allowing Shakespeare's autobiographical testimony to emerge."
Professor Daniel Wright
Director, Shakespeare Authorship Research Centre
Concordia University, Portland, OR

"Hank Whittemore clearly details the powerful evidence which proves beyond reasonable doubt that Edward de Vere created Shakespeare's Sonnets as a poetic monument to his son, Henry Wriothesley, 3rd Earl of Southampton."
Paul H. Altrocchi, MD
Author of *Most Greatly Lived*

"Finally, after 400 years, the Sonnets of Shake-Speare have found a worthy interpreter. Whittemore has been able to discover their original historical and political context and so reveal their true meaning."
Charles F. Beauclerk
Author of *Shakespeare's Lost Kingdom*

"I have studied this mystery for thirty-five years and Whittemore's discovery stands alone in its revelation of the structure and 'message in a bottle' of the Sonnets. I believe that with this key, he has unlocked the heart of these immortal poems."
K. C. Ligon
Actress, Playwright, Dialect Coach

"In our humble opinion, the truth uncovered by Whittemore has the capacity to determine the course of progressive Shakespeare studies for the next hundred years."
Carl S. Caruso
Author of *The Mystery of Hamlet*

D0840424

SHAKESPEARE'S SON

AND HIS SONNETS

An Expanded Introduction to

THE MONUMENT

by

Hank Whittemore

MARTIN AND LAWRENCE PRESS
GROTON, MASSACHUSETTS

Martin and Lawrence Press
PO Box 682
Groton, MA 01450

First Edition 2010
First Printing 2010

ISBN 9780982073216

Whittemore, Hank
Shakespeare's Son and his Sonnets

Library of Congress Control Number: 2010923130

Shakespeare, William. Sonnets / Sonnets, English – History and
Criticism / The Monument by Hank Whittemore / De Vere, Edward /
Oxford, seventeenth Earl of / L. H. (Hank) Whittemore / Shakespearean
Authorship

Cover Design by Sally Reed

Cover Art: Stained Glass Window in the
Medieval Parish Church in Felixstowe, Suffolk, England

Shakespeare's Son

"Even so my Sunne one early morn did shine
With all triumphant splendor on my brow,
But out alack, he was but one hour mine…"
                        Sonnet 33

"As a decrepit father takes delight
To see his active child do deeds of youth,
So I, made lame by Fortune's dearest spite,
Take all my comfort of thy worth and truth."
                        Sonnet 37

"O how thy worth with manners may I sing,
When thou art all the better part of me?"
                        Sonnet 39

"To you it doth belong
Your self to pardon of self-doing crime."
                        Sonnet 58

"Nativity, once in the main of light,
Crawls to maturity, wherewith being crowned,
Crooked eclipses 'gainst his glory fight…"
                        Sonnet 60

"And all those beauties whereof now he's King
Are vanishing, or vanished out of sight."
                        Sonnet 63

"Why should poor beauty indirectly seek
Roses of shadow, since his Rose is true?"
                        Sonnet 67

"If some suspect of ill masked not thy show,
Then thou alone kingdoms of hearts should'st owe"
                        Sonnet 70

ALSO BY THIS AUTHOR

THE MONUMENT *Shake-speare' Sonnets by Edward de Vere, 17th Earl of Oxford* — Meadow Geese Press, 2005

YOUR FUTURE SELF *A Journey to the Frontiers of the New Molecular Medicine* —Thames & Hudson, 1998

SO THAT OTHERS MAY LIVE *Caroline Hebard and Her Search & Rescue Dogs,* - Bantam, 1994

CNN: THE INSIDE STORY How a Band of Mavericks Changed the Face of TV News — Little, Brown, 1990

FIND THE MAGICIAN The *Counterfeiting Crime of the Century* — Viking, 1979

PEROFF: THE MAN WHO KNEW TOO MUCH *A True Story of Watergate* — Morrow, 1974

THE SUPER COPS *The True Story of the Cops Nicknamed Batman & Robin* — Stein & Day, 1973

TOGETHER *A Reporter's Journey into the New Black Politics* — Morrow, 1971

FEELING IT *A Novel* — Morrow, 1971

COP! *A Close-Up of Violence and Tragedy* — Holt, Rinehart 1969

THE MAN WHO RAN THE SUBWAYS *The Story of Mike Quill* - Holt, Rinehart - 1968

DEDICATION

To Glo

The Love of my Life

ACKNOWLEDGEMENTS

First I want to acknowledge the support of K.C. Ligon, whose death in 2009 left us all without her kindness, knowledge and wisdom.

I want to give special thanks to other friends and colleagues, regardless of differing viewpoints and conclusions about this subject matter, who contributed to this journey:

Paul Altrocchi, Mark Anderson, Mark Alexander, Steve Aucella (publisher of *The Monument*), Charles Beauclerk, Brian Bechtold, Charles (Chuck) Berney, Carole Berney, Dorna Bewley, Lee Boyd, Bill Boyle (who has made the journey with me), Charles Boyle (who introduced me to the Earl of Oxford), Michael Brame and Galina Popova Brame, Robert Brazil, James Brooks, Ralph Bucci, Albert Burgstahler, Barbara Burris, Pamela Butler, Stephanie Caruana, Carl Caruso, Michael Cecil, Derran Charlton, Matthew Cossolotto, Cynthia Crane, Barbara Crowley, Gordon Cyr, Bonner Miller Cutting, Michael Delahoyde, Richard Desper, Ron Destro, Robert Detobel, Peter Dickson, Lori DiLiddo, Cheryl Eagan Donovan, Ren Draya, Michael Dunn, Lee Durkee, Joseph Eldredge, Barboura Flues, Robin Fox, Gary Goldstein, Helen H. Gordon, Alan Green, Nina Green, Rima Greenhill, Donald Greenwood, Stanley Grill, Marguerite Gyatt, Janet Hamilton, Jim Hammond, Yolanda Hawkins, Ron Hess, Sandy Hochberg (research partner), Sylvia Crowley Holmes, Stephanie Hopkins Hughes, Tom Hunter, Mark Jackson, Ramon Jiminez, Richard Joyrich, Richard Kennedy, Lynne Kositsky, Michael Liguori, Carole Sue Lipman, Sundra Malcolm, Stuart Marlow, Jacquelyn Mason, Linda McLatchie, Alex McNeil (editor of *The Monument*), Ken Meece, Richard Meibers (publisher of *Shakespeare's Son and his Sonnets*), Marie Merkel, Jean Milgram, Roy and Lynn Morris, Donald Nelson, William Niederkorn, Eddy

Nix, James Norwood, Christopher Paul, Robert Prechter, Gerit Quealy, William Ray, Lisa Risley, Cynthia Ritsher, John Rollet, Marvin Rosenberg, Peter Rush, Mark Rylance, Sam Saunders, Jan Scheffer, Emily and Alfred Scott, Elisabeth [Betty] Sears (an early mentor), Mildred [Pidge] Sexton (a friend and supporter), John Shahan, Kathryn Sharpe, Loretta Sharpe, Wenonah Sharpe, Randall Sherman, Sherwood, Karyn Sherwood, Earl and Lee Showerman, Richard Smiley, Elliot Stone, Ted Story (co-writer and director of the one-man show *Shake-speare's Treason*, based on *The Monument*), Roger Stritmatter, Paul Streitz, Linda Taylor, Linda Theil, Mary Tooze, John and Pat Urquhart, John Varady, Bill Varble, Richard Whalen, Heward Wilkinson, Clive Willingham, Laura Wilson, Lisa Wilson, John Wood, Daniel Wright and Rick Wyckoff.

Also my special thanks to Bob Arietta, Ed Coury, Peter and Thelma Huber, Sue Smith, Jen Hatch and Jack Winkopp.

I want to send my love and thanks to my parents, Bill and Suzette Whittemore, along with my brothers and sisters: Bill, Jim, Suzanne, Richard and Marianne; my children: Eva, Lorna, Ben, Maggie and Jake; my grandchildren: Nicole and Thomas; my son-in-law Adam Lowry; my brother-in-law Chris Janata, his wife Leslie and their children Milo and Quinn. Special love and thanks to my mother-in-law Maddy Janata and my father-in-law Jerry Janata, who have always encouraged me.

Thanks and love to the Aguilar family: Efrain, Yolanda, Chris and Jimmy.

And once again I dedicate this book with love to Gloria Janata-Whittemore, my amazing and wonderful wife, who brings joy and love wherever she goes.

Table of Contents

INTRODUCTION

Welcome to this adventure into SHAKE-SPEARES SONNETS, the sequence of 154 numbered verses printed in 1609, which have been referred to as "the greatest puzzle in the history of English literature." This artistic masterwork has thrilled and moved millions of readers for centuries, but the verses have been an enigma in terms of their meaning as well as their relationship to the author's life and contemporary history. In these pages based on my 900-page edition *The Monument*, I would like to offer a new way of reading the Sonnets that brings them alive as a true story of political intrigue, passion, betrayal and, ultimately, the end of the Tudor dynasty as recorded in a clandestine diary.

My hope is that, no matter what you think of the conclusions expressed here, you'll come away with an increased appreciation of the poems; and for young scholars setting forth into classrooms to teach the works of Shakespeare, here's another perspective to offer students as they look at the Sonnets and begin to explore them.

The Monument was the result of unexpected discoveries. I had begun my journey as a playwright, author and actor with great love for Shakespeare and many unanswered questions about the genesis of his knowledge and motivation to write the plays and narrative poems and, most particularly, the tortured autobiography of the Sonnets. Starting with a series of assumptions and hypotheses, based on both my own and others' interpretations, I conducted a series of tests that led unexpectedly to a paradigm-changing view of the language, structure and chronology of the 154-sonnet sequence, not to mention the actual content of the poems. Suddenly the pieces of the puzzle began to move by themselves into place, so that all I had to do was watch them fit together to form a clear picture.

For me one of the most startling aspects of this new paradigm is the existence of 100 chronologically arranged sonnets (a "century") at the center of an elegant structure or design:

• Exactly eighty sonnets of the Fair Youth series (1-126) or more than half the full sequence of 154 sonnets are written to and/or about Henry Wriothesley, Third Earl of Southampton (1573?-1624), the younger man known to us as the Fair Youth, during the two years from 1601 to 1603 when he was imprisoned in the Tower of London as a traitor.

• Immediately following this block are twenty more sonnets addressed to Southampton, who, following the death of Queen Elizabeth on March 24, 1603, was suddenly and inexplicably released from prison by the newly proclaimed King James I of England.

• The additional twenty sonnets begin with Southampton's liberation by James on April 10, 1603 and conclude with the funeral of Elizabeth on April 28, 1603, marking the end of the 118-year Tudor dynasty on the English throne.

The new historical context is confirmed in the Sonnets by specific, recorded events surrounding Southampton's imprisonment and release; further, when studied from the standpoint of their structure, the 100 sonnets at the center support the conclusion that the author deliberately erected a "monument" of verse for Henry Wriothesley, to whom he promised:

So long as men can breathe or eyes can see,
So long lives this, and this gives life to thee.
                    Sonnet 18

Since these findings came into view, I have often wished they could be presented strictly on their own terms, without the implications they necessarily raise about the author, his relationship to

Southampton as the Fair Youth and the true political history of the Elizabethan reign. Sometimes a basic solution to a problem can trigger such heated debate over its ramifications that the solution itself is discarded along with its postulates. The point here is that regardless of these implications, all the elements of the sonnets can be seen at last as working in harmony and without contradiction – something that has not been possible before now.

Many suggestions by others in the past turn out to be correct; added to these are facts based on actual dates of events, consistent translations of frequently used words and an overwhelming amount of new circumstantial evidence. These all lead to reasonable conclusions regarding the longstanding mystery surrounding the Sonnets. as well as revealing the true identity of their elusive author.

First this work confirms that Southampton is the younger man addressed in Sonnets 1-126 and the primary subject of all the other verses (127-154) as well. The monument is for him and him alone. (He is "the onlie begetter" who inspired the Sonnets, thereby giving birth to them, as stated in the cryptic dedication.) The implications also lead to the inescapable conclusion that Elizabeth I of England (1533-1603) is the powerful, deceitful Sovereign Mistress known as the Dark Lady who is the addressee of Sonnets 127-152.

The crucial result of the Monument Theory is the context of time and circumstance: Elizabeth was keeping the Southampton in her royal prison fortress for playing a lead role in the failed Essex Rebellion of February 8, 1601; and the author's personal reaction to this tragedy led him to write and compile the central sequence of 100 intensely wrought verses that would become the centerpiece of the Sonnets.

Once the stencil of time and circumstance is laid over the collection, the verses can be read as a contemporary record of actual events; and what unfolds is a dramatic, flesh-and-blood story that challenges interpretations of both the history and the literature. The story also confirms that the world's greatest writer actually lived the experiences that he wrote about, much in the way that Mark Twain, Ernest Hemingway, Arthur Miller and Tennessee Williams provide windows into their personal lives and even into the politics of their day.

Edward de Vere, Seventeenth Earl of Oxford (1550-1604) was hereditary Lord Great Chamberlain of England and the most illustrious patron of the arts during the Elizabethan reign. Educated by the finest tutors from boyhood, he received honorary degrees from Cambridge and Oxford before studying law at Gray's Inn. A writer for the stage, he was known as "best for comedy" and deemed the "most excellent" of the courtier poets.

Oxford had a volatile relationship with Queen Elizabeth and her chief minister, William Cecil, Lord Treasurer Burghley, who was also his father-in-law. Based on the contents of the Sonnets, I contend (as others have in the past) that Oxford was the Queen's lover in the early 1570s and that, by her, he fathered the boy raised as Henry Wriothesley, Third Earl of Southampton, who was therefore the rightful heir to the throne. This relationship of father and royal son explains the tone and urgency of the Sonnets while shedding light on heretofore unexplainable events of history that led up to, and immediately followed, the Queen's death in the spring of 1603.

In fact Oxford was the highest-ranking earl on the jury of peers at the trial of Southampton and Robert Devereux, Second Earl of Essex, on February 19, 1601. After having to condemn his son to death, he labored under extreme pressure to find a way to save him. "Thy adverse party is thy Advocate," he tells Southampton in Sonnet 35, on the eve of the treason trial, and proceeds to make a bargain with Burghley's son and successor, Secretary Robert Cecil, requiring him to bury the truth about his own and England's history.

After winning the power struggle behind the throne, Secretary Cecil made sure Essex went to his execution and then held

Southampton hostage in the Tower until the Queen's death and the peaceful succession of James, thereby retaining his power in the new reign. The underlying truth of this story was kept out of the historical record; but Oxford, by means of the "dynastic" diary of the Sonnets, produced a monument for Southampton to preserve "the living record of your memory" that contains the truth of what really happened; and like a message in a bottle, it was set adrift on the sea of time in the hope it would make its way to the distant shores of posterity.

"Who will believe my verse in time to come," he wonders in Sonnet 17, addressing Southampton as his royal son, "if it were filled with your most high deserts?" And he predicts in the same verse that "your true rights" to the throne will be "termed a Poet's rage and stretched meter of an Antique song" – a forecast that has proved all too accurate, for far too long.

On May 7, 1603, just ten days after the funeral of the Queen had marked the "official" end of the Tudor dynasty, and when the chronology of Oxford's diary had ended, he wrote to Secretary Robert Cecil and reminded him:

"But I hope truth is subject to no prescription, for truth is truth though never so old, and time cannot make that false which was once true."

The cunning Secretary had forced Oxford to sacrifice his identity, both as the father of the Queen's heir and as the author of the "Shakespeare" works that he had dedicated publicly to Southampton – who had to renounce his claim of succession in return for his life and freedom and a royal pardon. Reminding Cecil that "truth is truth" until the end of time, however, Oxford was telling him in effect:

"You're the winner and therefore you get to write the history, but I've set down what really happened and your false official version will never be able to erase it. This truth is preserved in a monument for 'eyes not yet created,' and, in the end, it will be triumphant."

Such is the solemn promise that Oxford made to Southampton in Sonnet 81:

> Your monument shall be my gentle verse,
> Which eyes not yet created shall o'er-read,
> And tongues to be your being shall rehearse,
> When all the breathers of this world are dead.
> You still shall live (such virtue hath my Pen)
> Where breath most breathes, even in the mouths of men.

I trust the following pages convey my reverence for the extraordinary masterwork of the Sonnets – for the beauty and power of the verses, as well as for the duality that allows them to be both universal and specific at the same time. My experience has convinced me that, far from diminishing our ability to appreciate these poems, knowing the real-life story only serves to increase our recognition of their value on every level.

Chapter One

A ROYAL STORY

On May 20, 1609, the Stationers' Register in London recorded the intention of Thomas Thorpe to publish "a Booke called Shakespeares sonnettes." Below is a depiction of the title page as it appears on four of the thirteen surviving copies. (Seven other recovered copies indicate that the book was "to be solde by John Wright, dwelling at Christ Church gate"; two more lack title pages.) It was common practice for the author of a work to be named in between the two parallel lines; but on the title page for the Sonnets, this space was left conspicuously blank:

SHAKE-SPEARES
SONNETS

Never Before Imprinted

AT LONDON
By G. Eld for T.T. and are
To be solde by William Aspley.
1609

A cryptic dedication was printed inside, in the form of three upside-down pyramids:

TO. THE. ONLIE. BEGETTER. OF.
THESE. ENSUING. SONNETS.
Mr. W. H. ALL. HAPPINESSE.
AND. THAT. ETERNITIE.
PROMISED.
BY.
OUR. EVER-LIVING. POET.
WISHETH.
THE. WELL-WISHING.
ADVENTURER. IN.
SETTING.
FORTH.

T.T.

The quarto volume (known to us as Q) promptly fell into a resounding silence, without a single authentic contemporary reference to its existence. (A note on a letter to actor Edward Alleyn of June 19, 1609, recording the purchase of Shaksper sonetts, is "almost certainly a forgery by John Payne Collier," writes Katherine Duncan-Jones)

Scholar Frank Mathew suggested in 1922: "The neglect of the Sonnets of 1609 can only be explained by concluding they were quickly suppressed."

Most of the thirteen original copies that have been recovered are very clean, suggesting they hadn't been widely read or circulated; so it's possible the book was never intended for the public and, instead, tucked into private libraries to be rediscovered by readers of future generations.

A bogus collection in 1640 contained all but eight of the original sonnets; these were printed out of order and merged to form longer poems under made-up titles; and in a few instances, the gender of the Fair Youth was changed from male to female; but the authentic publication of 1609 remained unnoticed for more than a century, until a surviving copy was reproduced in 1711. By the eighteenth century, the truth recorded in the verses was hidden by preconceptions about "Shakespeare" that had grown to the magnitude of legend, so the real story continued to hide in plain sight.

For the diary of the Sonnets to reveal itself and come alive, readers of the future would need to know the personal, political and historical context in which it was written. And at some point they would have to find the true author.

"William Shakespeare" had made his triumphant entrance onto the printed page by dedicating *Venus and Adonis* of 1593 as "the first heir of my invention" to Henry Wriothesley. He had followed this with *The Rape of Lucrece of 1594*, again for Southampton, pledging in the second public letter:

"The love I dedicate to your Lordship is without end … What I have done is yours, what I have to do is yours; being part in all I have, devoted yours."

Nichol Smith stated in 1916: "There is no other dedication like this in Elizabethan literature."

The poet never dedicated another work, thereby uniquely associating Henry Wriothesley with his name; but the lack of any connection between the traditionally assumed biography of "Shakespeare" and the life of Southampton has meant, as Smith deduced, that "further proofs of their friendship must be sought in the Sonnets."

"The real problem of the Sonnets is to find out who 'Shakespeare' was," Sir George Greenwood dared to write in 1908. "That done, it might be possible to make the crooked straight and the rough places plane – but not till then."

But once we put aside the legendary image and try to discover the author based on what he wrote in these verses, our picture of him altogether changes, leading Sir Greenwood to conclude: "That he would be found among cultivated Elizabethan courtiers of high position, I have no doubt."

When British schoolmaster John Thomas Looney described his new theory of Edward de Vere's authorship of the Shakespeare works in 1920, he reported the earl had written the earliest sonnet or "little song" of the Elizabethan reign (circa 1573) in the form to be used much later by "Shakespeare" and subsequently called the "Shakespearean" form. (Fourteen lines created by three quatrains plus a final couplet, with a rhyme scheme abab cdcd efef gg, each line having ten beats.) Oxford wrote his sonnet (entitled *Love Thy Choice)* soon after entering Court at twenty-one in 1571, expressing his loyalty to the Queen, then in her thirty-eighth year. He did so by asking himself a series of rhetorical questions, the answer to each of which is "Elizabeth":

Who taught thee first to sigh, alas, my heart?
Who taught thy tongue the woeful words of plaint?
Who filled your eyes with tears of bitter smart?
Who gave thee grief and made thy joys to faint?
Who first did paint with colors pale thy face?
Who first did break thy sleeps of quiet rest?
Above the rest in Court who gave thee grace?
Who made thee strive in honor to be best?
In constant truth to bide so firm and sure,
To scorn the world regarding but thy friends?
With patient mind each passion to endure,
In one desire to settle to the end?
Love then thy choice wherein such choice doth bind,
As nought but death may ever change thy mind.

The poet of the Shakespeare sonnets "assumes the attitude of a matured man addressing a youth," Looney pointed out, observing he appears to indicate his age as "forty winters" in the first seventeen sonnets, when the poet was urging the seventeen-year-old Earl of Southampton to quickly marry and perpetuate his blood line; and those opening verses "are assigned generally to about the year 1590, when Oxford was just forty years of age."

Oxford was "a nobleman of the same high rank as Southampton and just a generation older," Looney wrote, adding that "the peculiar circumstances of the youth to whom the Sonnets were addressed were strikingly analogous to his own."

• Edward de Vere became the first royal ward of Elizabeth at age twelve in 1562, under the guardianship of William Cecil (later Lord Burghley), and in 1571 he entered into an arranged marriage with the chief minister's fifteen-year-old daughter, Anne Cecil.

• Henry Wriothesley became the eighth and last "child of state" as a boy in 1581, also in the chief minister's custody, and during 1590-91 he resisted unusual pressure to enter into an arranged marriage with Burghley's fifteen-year-old granddaughter, Elizabeth Vere.

"Both had been left orphans and royal wards at an early age, both had been brought up under the same guardian, both had the same kind of literary tastes and interests, and later the young man followed exactly the same course as the elder as a patron of literature and drama. Then, just at the time when these sonnets were being written urging Southampton to marry, he was actually being urged into a marriage with a daughter of the Earl of Oxford.

"To find so reasonable a key, then, to a set of sonnets on so peculiar a theme is something in itself, and to find this key so directly connected with the very man we had selected as the probable author of the poems is almost disconcerting in its conclusiveness."

The separate entries for Oxford and Southampton in the *Dictionary of National Biography* reveal that "in many of its leading features the life of the younger man is a reproduction of the life of the elder," Looney noted, so it was "difficult to resist the feeling that Wriothesley had made a hero of De Vere, and had attempted to model his life on that of his predecessor as royal ward."

Southampton stood firm against all pressures to marry Elizabeth Vere, so the Queen and Burghley abandoned the idea, and after sonnets 1–17 the poet dropped his insistence without looking back. However, judging by the private verses that followed in the Fair Youth series (Sonnets 1-126), the two men shared a much closer and deeper bond.

Writing to Henry Wriothesley in Sonnet 37, the poet likens himself to "a decrepit father who takes delight to see his active child do deeds of youth," adding that he derives "all my comfort of thy worth and truth." In Sonnet 39 he says Southampton is "all the better part of me" and in Sonnet 48 he refers to him as "mine only care." He wonders in Sonnet 108 what else "may express my love, or thy dear merit," answering, "Nothing, sweet boy, but yet like prayers divine, I must each day say o'er the very same, counting no old thing old, thou mine, I thine, even as when first I hallowed thy fair name."

Southampton is "abundant issue" in Sonnet 97, as well as "but hope of Orphans, and un-fathered fruit." He is "a God in love, to whom I am confined" in Sonnet 110. "If my dear love were but the child of state," the poet says of him in Sonnet 124, "it might for fortune's bastard be un-fathered." In Sonnet 125 he offers his "oblation" or religious sacrifice to him as a deity; and at the end of the series, Sonnet 126, he cries out: "O Thou my lovely Boy, who in thy power dost hold time's fickle glass, his sickle hour, who hast by waning grown…"

It would seem that knowing who "Shakespeare" really was means knowing who Southampton really was.

The Monument (2005) resulted from new observations about the Sonnets that emerged during the winter of 1998-1999, after more than a dozen years of research into the life of Edward de Vere and his relationship to the "Shakespeare" works. There was strong evidence of his authorship, but still unanswered was why he adopted the pen name in connection with Southampton in 1593 and then why, upon his death in 1604, the year *Hamlet* was published, he joined the Prince in leaving a "wounded name" and "things standing thus unknown" behind a curtain of silence. And why did others continue to conceal the truth about him?

If the traditional biography of William Shakespeare was a "Big Lie," what "Big Truth" lay behind it? Surely there had been a motive powerful enough to produce the greatest literary hoax in history.

By then I was well acquainted with the view of some past Oxfordians (notably Percy Allen in the 1930s and Dorothy and Charlton Ogburn in the 1950s), who believed that Edward de Vere and Elizabeth were the parents of an unacknowledged royal son raised as Henry Wriothesley, Third Earl of Southampton. A crucial aspect of this theory was that Oxford and Elizabeth must have gone through a private betrothal ceremony, when she vowed to name their son as her successor, King Henry IX.

In that case the Big Lie of "Shakespeare" is explained as having been perpetrated to further conceal the Big Truth that the "Virgin Queen," who never married or gave birth, did in fact have a legitimate heir. The government would have had to conceal this fact at any cost, even if it also meant having to obliterate the identity of the greatest writer of the English language, who had used the warrior-like pen name "Shakespeare" as a political weapon to publicly support his royal son. The same Big Lie also would have been perpetrated to prevent civil war around the throne occupied from 1603 to 1625 by King James, not to mention succeeding monarchs.

Preposterous? Yes, even to other Oxfordians. Mind-boggling? Yes, but as Sherlock Holmes says: "When you have eliminated the impossible, whatever remains, however improbable, must be the truth…"

As the twentieth century drew to a close, all other explanations had fallen short; only this "Prince Tudor" theory, however improbable, appeared to be the truth. And if a record of this truth existed, it seemed to me, the place to find it would be in the Sonnets.

The great mistake, I felt, was viewing these intensely autobiographical poems only or primarily as literature, when they are meant to be perceived as entries of a diary recording real events in real time.

My hypotheses included the Shakespeare sonnets as autobiographical and, within each series, arranged by the poet in chronological order. To me it was clear the verses are nonfiction dressed as fiction, adding up to a genuine historical document; and beyond that, in my view, this unique sequence of poems must have been Shakespeare's *magnum opus* in terms of what he wanted us to know about his life.

I was not alone in reading the verses as addressed to a prince; the only way to avoid such an impression was to ignore it. Professor G. W. Knight observes: "The Sonnets are the heart of Shakespeare's royal poetry … The loved one is royal … He is 'crowned' with various gifts of Nature and Fortune, especially 'all those beauties whereof now he's King.' Like a 'sovereign,' he radiates 'worth', his eyes lending a 'double majesty'…"

With the traditional Shakespeare legend as his operating reality, Knight necessarily viewed these allusions as metaphorical; but Leslie Hotson, also an orthodox scholar, nevertheless declared in 1964 that the poet was addressing the younger man literally as his sovereign:

"Shakespeare typifies his Friend variously as a Sun, a God, an Ocean or a Sea: three familiar metaphors which he and his contemporaries use to represent a sovereign prince or king ... What he sets before us is not the powers of a peer, but those peculiar to a king: power to grant charters of privilege and letters patent, power to pardon crimes – in short, the exclusively royal prerogative...

"Clearly, these consenting terms cannot be dismissed as scattered surface-ornament. They are intrinsic. What is more, they intensify each other.

"By direct address, by varied metaphor and by multifarious allusion, the description of the Friend communicated is always one: monarch, sovereign prince, king. The poet's harping on the same string is so insistent as to make one ask why it has not arrested attention. No doubt everyone has regarded this 'king sense' as formal hyperbole and nothing more. Any literal meaning looks quite incredible, a rank impossibility..."

Hotson was well acquainted with the evidence of Southampton as the Fair Youth, so he found himself sternly lecturing:

"Sustained and unmistakable, this language of Shakespeare's lends no support to the common theory that his youthful Friend might be some nobleman or other. For it is obvious that his chosen terms point not to nobility, but to royalty."

Anyone perceiving that Henry Wriothesley, Earl of Southampton was in fact an unacknowledged prince raised as a nobleman may be forgiven for smiling at the irony of Hotson's argument!

Charlton Ogburn Jr. sums up the problem:

"We are left with a compelling question raised by the Sonnets. It is a question that is inescapable and one that traditional scholarship is resolved upon escaping at all costs. How is it that the poet of the Sonnets can – as he unmistakably does – address the Fair Youth as an adoring and deeply concerned father would address his son and as a subject would his liege-lord?"

Chapter Two

A SPECIAL LANGUAGE

The language, structure, attitude, tone and content of the Sonnets all lead to and support the theory that Lord Southampton was the unacknowledged royal son of Queen Elizabeth I and Lord Oxford. What appears on the surface as the story of a "love triangle" (involving the author in relation to his dominating Mistress and his beloved Friend) can also be viewed consistently as Edward de Vere's dangerous political and historical document about the right of Henry Wriothesley to succeed the Sovereign Mistress of England on the throne as King Henry IX – in other words, a "family triangle" involving Oxford and the Queen as parents and Southampton as royal son with a royal claim.

By law, asserting any claim of succession was an act of treason, so Oxford would have been forced to be indirect, as he writes in Sonnet 66: "And art made tongue-tied by authority."

"This autobiography is written by a foreign man in a foreign tongue, which can never be translated," T. S. Eliot concluded about the Sonnets in 1927; but the poet tells us that because he cannot be open and forthright he has created an "invention" or special language to produce a kind of double image: creating a fictional story that appears on the surface while recording his true story at the same time. Each word produces two separate, overlapping images. At the same time he keeps "dressing old words new" (exchanging one word for another to mean the same thing) within the "noted weed" or familiar costume of poetry:

Why write I still all one, ever the same,
And keep invention in a noted weed…

So all my best is dressing old words new,
Spending again what is already spent.
    Sonnet 76

His special language consists of words that all revolve around the three members of the family triangle, within which Southampton is the "one" who should be king:

Fair, kind, and true, is all my argument,
Fair, kind, and true, varying to other words,
And in this change is my invention spent,
Three themes in one, which wondrous scope affords.
    Sonnet 105

This Written Ambassage

He refers to the poetical sequence of the Sonnets as an "ambassage" or secret document intended for a monarch; in this case, intended for his royal son:

Lord of my love, to whom in vassalage
Thy merit hath my duty strongly knit,
To thee I send this written ambassage,
To witness duty, not to show my wit.
    Sonnet 26

An ambassador usually memorized his highly sensitive, official message and delivered it orally to a prince. Presumably if captured he would endure torture to the death without revealing his highly sensitive and dangerous, secret communication. Oxford, of course, needed to use words on the page to conceal and reveal his message for his royal son, so his ambassage to a prince had to be a "written" one.

Beauty's Rose

Opening the Fair Youth series, Oxford uses the royal "we" to command "fairest creatures" (royal children) to beget "increase" (heirs) to ensure that "beauty's *Rose*" (Elizabeth's Tudor Rose dynasty) might not end upon her death:

> From fairest creatures we desire increase,
> That thereby beauty's *Rose* might never die
>   Sonnet 1

These lines announce the beginning of a dynastic diary:

> "From royal sons the Queen and I command heirs,
> So her Tudor Rose Dynasty might not perish"

From here on in the diary, we can view Edward de Vere as consistently using "fair" for Southampton's royalty and "beauty" for Elizabeth as well as for the Tudor blood line or lineage that he inherited from her.

Queen Elizabeth was often referred to as "Beauty" and "Beauty's Rose" could not fail to echo the Tudor Rose dynasty begun by her grandfather, Henry VII, in 1485.

Beauty's Successive Heir

Her Majesty's imperial viewpoint determined everything; her favor was a beacon of light upon her subjects, while her frown was a dark cloud casting its shadow upon the world. Elizabeth's disgrace of her royal son is what turns him from "fair" to "black" in the opening of the Dark Lady series:

In the old age black was not counted fair,
Or if it were it bore not beauty's name,
But now is black beauty's successive heir,
And beauty slandered with a bastard shame.
    Sonnet 127

Or to paraphrase:
"Earlier our disgraced son was not counted royal,
  Or if he was, he bore not Elizabeth's name of Tudor,
  But now he is still her immediate successor,
  And she slanders him with the stain of bastardy."

The Double Image
The double image of the Sonnets is similar to that of a composite picture depicting a flock of birds in the sky and also a school of fish in the water. To produce this effect, the artist has drawn every line in the service of both images, so whether one or the other is observed depends upon a viewer's perception, based on prior information and experience. Could Oxford have written every word of the Sonnets in the service of two images at once?

All One, Ever the Same
He answers this exactly in Sonnet 76, starting with:
Why write I still *all one, ever the same*
He keeps recording a single topic, which is always the same; and in the same five words he identifies the principals of this subtext running in parallel with the surface image:

All One
Henry Wriothsley, 3rd Earl of Southampton
    His motto ONE FOR ALL, ALL FOR ONE
Ever the Same
Elizabeth Tudor, Queen Elizabeth I

Her motto EVER THE SAME

This is the central key: the subject matter of the Sonnets is figuratively and literally "all one, ever the same" or Southampton in relation to Queen Elizabeth; and the author, Oxford, is recording the progress of this particular story as it unfolds in real life:

Ever

Edward de Vere, 17th Earl of Oxford
    His name E. VER

All in One

In 1859, a researcher identified only as "W. C. J." was first to observe the pervasive presence of Southampton's motto in the Sonnets, adding that the words and theme of the phrase "all one, ever the same" had been "adapted in different ways, with considerable poetic and idiosyncratic license," such as:

Resembling sire, and child, and happy mother,
Who *all in one*, one pleasing note do sing.
    Sonnet 8

Charlotte Stopes declared: "Shakespeare's poems, dedications, and Sonnets were all to one patron and one friend, and that one was Henry Wriothesley third Earl of Southampton."

She added that his family motto is echoed in:

Since *all alike* my songs and praises be
To one, of one, still such, and ever so
    Sonnet 105

Nothing Truer than Truth

Oxford's earldom motto *Vero Nihil Verius* (*Nothing Truer than Truth*) exists throughout the sonnets:

Thou *truly* fair wert *truly* sympathized
In *true* plain words by thy *true*-telling friend
    Sonnet 82

Ever or Never

An early pen name of Edward de Vere had been Ever or Never. He often played upon his name as "ever" and "every" along with "never":

O no, it is an *ever*-fixed mark
That looks on tempests and is *never* shaken;
It is the star to *every* wandering bark...
If this be error and upon me proved,
I *never* writ, nor no man *ever* loved.
    Sonnet 116

We can hear Oxford insist on himself ("every") and Southampton ("one") as linked together — as when both must suffer beneath the "shadow" of disgrace cast by the monarch's frown and her withdrawal of royal favor:

What is your substance, whereof are you made,
That millions of strange shadows on you tend?
Since *every one* hath, *every one, one* shade,
And you, but *one,* can *every* shadow lend
    Sonnet 53

Every Word

Edward de Vere restricts his topic to Southampton and Elizabeth, never wavering; but at the same time, his "invention" employs the "noted weed" or familiar costume of poetry, enabling him to use "every word" to "almost" reveal his own "name" or identity and record his story, from its "birth" to where it has managed to "proceed" (issue from the womb) in this diary:

> Why write I still all one, ever the same
> And keep invention in a noted weed,
> That every word doth almost tell my name,
> Showing their birth, and where they did proceed?
> Sonnet 76

You and Love

Southampton carries the blood of both parents, so the actual topic of "all one, ever the same" is him and his "love" or inherited royal blood:

> O know, sweet love, I always write of you,
> And you and love are still my argument
> Sonnet 76

Dressing Old Words New

Given this severe restriction, the best the author can do is keep "dressing old words new" or substituting words to consistently refer to the same thing:

> So all my best is dressing old words new,
> Spending again what is already spent
> Sonnet 76

In this perspective, Oxford deliberately uses simple, familiar words such as *fair, beauty, Rose, love, one, all, ever, never, truth* and *true* to help create his double image.

Truth and Beauty

In Sonnet 14 he refers to himself as Truth and to Elizabeth as Beauty, urging Henry Wriothesley to "convert" from his stubborn course and prevent the "doom" of their hopes:

> As truth and beauty shall together thrive,
> If from thy self to store thou wouldst convert:
> Or else of thee this I prognosticate,
> Thy end is Truth's and Beauty's doom and date.
> Sonnet 14

It would be fatuous to predict the end of Truth and Beauty as universal concepts, but Shakespeare was never fatuous. On the non-fiction level, without hyperbole, these lines state that Southampton's untimely death would dash his parents' hopes for a dynastic future.

Oxford later demonstrates how he keeps "dressing old words new" or "varying to other words" to create an appearance of variety. Again he restricts himself to the family triangle and the "one" royal son who embodies it:

He cites three different words used for the same topic:

> Fair, kind, and true, is all my argument,
> Fair, kind, and true, varying to other words,
> And in this change is my invention spent,
> Three themes in one, which wondrous scope affords
> Sonnet 105

Your True Rights

The final sonnet of the "marriage and propagation" sequence acquires new meaning and power in this perspective. Ending his plea for Southampton to enter a Cecil family alliance, Oxford expresses doubt that future readers will comprehend his intended meaning:

> Who will believe my verse in time to come
> If it were filled with your most high deserts?
>> Sonnet 17

He predicts they will see only the conventional, outdated poetry:

> So should my papers (yellowed with their age)
> Be scorned, like old men of less truth than tongue,
> And your true rights be termed a Poet's rage
> And stretched meter of an Antique song.
>> Sonnet 17

His forecast was accurate. Four hundred years later, most readers still fail to recognize the "true rights" of Henry Wriothesley to be King Henry IX of England.

Chapter Three

A DYNAMIC DESIGN

The monument built for Southampton is not for the contemporary world, but for "eyes not yet created" in future generations, including our own:

> Your monument shall be my gentle verse,
> Which eyes not yet created shall o'er-read
>> Sonnet 81

> And thou in this shalt find thy monument,
> When tyrants' crests and tombs of brass are spent.
>> Sonnet 107

Eternal Numbers

Its structure is put together by the arrangement of the 154 "numbers" of the sequence:

> And in fresh numbers number all your graces
>> Sonnet 17

> Eternal numbers to outlive long date
>> Sonnet 38

Time's Pyramids

The monument of the Sonnets is constructed as a pyramid; but each of the 154 numbered sonnets is also a "pyramid" measuring the Time that forms the chronology of the diary:

No! Time, thou shalt not boast that I do change!
Thy pyramids built up with newer might
To me are nothing novel, nothing strange,
They are but dressings of a former sight.
     Sonnet 123

The individual pyramids (sonnets) mark specific dates on the calendar, in terms of years or months or days; and just as Oxford is "dressing old words new" to create diversity, so the actual sonnets are "dressings of a former sight" to record the same story.

The Tomb

The monument of the Sonnets is similar in its intention to the ancient Egyptian pyramids, constructed as tombs to preserve dynastic rulers (pharaohs) until they attained eternal life. The tomb of the Sonnets is constructed with words intended to both conceal and reveal the truth:

Who will believe my verse in time to come
If it were filled with your most high deserts?
Though yet heaven knows it is but as a tomb
Which hides your life, and shows not half your parts
     Sonnet 17

The Womb

Oxford used a familiar Elizabethan image of the poet in relation to his poem as a parent in relation to his child; but he extends this notion by the conceit that his diary itself is a "womb" giving rebirth to his son, thereby enabling him and his royal blood to grow. His thoughts, expressed in the words of an ongoing chronicle or diary, have been made to undergo a transformation:

Making their tomb the womb wherein they grew
     Sonnet 86

The Living Record

The result of Southampton's rebirth and growth, by means of this womb of words and thoughts, is "the living record" or diary of his life and truth to be preserved for readers of posterity:

> Nor Mars his sword nor war's quick fire shall burn
> The living record of your memory.
> 'Gainst death and all oblivious enmity
> Shall you pace forth! Your praise shall still find room
> Even in the eyes of all posterity
> That wear this world out to the ending doom.
>   Sonnet 55

Structure

Oxford built the monument not from the outside, but from the inside, at what is now its center. The surrounding segments, added later, are scaffolding. What we see at first is the final product of 154 sonnets, of which virtually all scholars have identified three fundamental parts:

Fair Youth	**Sonnets 1-126**	**(126 sonnets)**
Dark Lady	**Sonnets 127-152**	**(26 sonnets)**
Bath Visit	**Sonnets 153-154**	**(2 sonnets)**

This "table of contents" is correct, but it obscures the elegant monument.

Epilogue: Sonnets 153-154

The two final sonnets refer to the visit of the Queen and her Court to the City of Bath in August 1574, the year of Southampton's birth. Sonnets 153-154 represent Oxford's infant son by Elizabeth as "Cupid" and "The Boy" who is also called "The Little Love-God" at the beginning of his life. Therefore this epilogue is actually the prologue of the "living record" of Southampton and belongs at the top of the pyramidal structure.

Bath Visit
153-154
(2 sonnets)

Dark Lady
127------------------152
(26 sonnets)

Fair Youth
1-- 126
(126 sonnets)

ENVOYS: SONNETS 26 & 126

SONNET 126, addressed to "My Lovely Boy," is the envoy or postscript to the Fair Youth Series.

SONNET 26, a recognized dedicatory epistle addressed to "Lord of My Love," is also an envoy ending a sequence.

Sonnets 26 and 126 are the two most important pillars of the monument, dividing its foundation or base into three sections with precisely 100 sonnets at the center:

"Lord of My Love"   "My Lovely Boy"
/   /
1---------26   27------------------126   127----------152
(26 sonnets)   *(100 sonnets)*   *(26 sonnets)*

The 100-Sonnet Center

The 100 sequential and chronological verses from Sonnet 27 to

Sonnet 126 are the heart of "the living record" of Southampton, serving as the center and centerpiece of the monument.

A precedent was *A Hundredth Sundrie Flowres* of 1573, containing exactly 100 verses in its mix of prose and poetry — a collection with which Oxford has been associated as the most likely writer as well as editor and publisher. Another precedent was *The Hekatompathia or The Passionate Century of Love* of 1582, with exactly 100 consecutively numbered verses dedicated by Thomas Watson to Oxford, again the more likely author.

The Center

I will find where truth is hid,
Though it were hid indeed within the center
Hamlet, 2.2.171

Oxford describes his "invention" at the exact midpoint, Sonnets 76-77, the entranceway into the monument.

27-------------76   77-------------126
(50 sonnets)   *(50 sonnets)*

SONNET 76 explains "my verse" of the Sonnets.

SONNET 77 dedicates "this book" to Southampton.

Oxford begins Sonnet 76 by describing the womb of "my verse" as increasingly "barren." He testifies that in writing these sonnets he continually uses just one method, which involves "compounds" of words similar to the chemical mixtures in alchemy. Meanwhile the crucial information of the opening quatrain is that he writes "with the time," as in an ongoing diary.

Why is my verse so barren of new pride?
So far from variation or quick change?
Why with the time do I not glance aside
To new-found methods, and to compounds strange?
    Sonnet 76

Dynamics

The Sonnets tell the story of LOVE struggling against the tyranny of TIME:

And all in war with Time for love of you...
    Sonnet 15

THE SONNETS = LOVE VS. TIME

LOVE = SOUTHAMPTON
TIME = ELIZABETH

TIME is the ever-dwindling life and reign of Elizabeth, leading to her death and the question of succession, which will determine the fate of the Tudor dynasty.

TIME, in all its various manifestations, is literally and dynamically the TIME LINE of the diary or chronicle of the Sonnets; and therefore, the story being recorded is that of Southampton and his royal blood struggling to survive the ever-waning time left in the life, reign and dynasty of Elizabeth:

But wherefore do not you a mightier way
Make war upon this bloody tyrant time?
    Sonnet 15

Oxford knows the diary will end upon the death of the Queen and the date with the succession, when the fate of her dynasty will be sealed. Writing and compiling his entries in real time, however, he can predict neither the precise moment of her death nor the circumstances that will prevail when she expires. The story has two possible outcomes:

• Southampton's LOVE wins the race with TIME when he is named to succeed Elizabeth upon her death, or

• Southampton's LOVE loses the race with TIME when the Queen dies and he fails to become King Henry IX.

The actual word TIME appears seventy-eight times in the Fair Youth series 1–126, but nowhere else in the collection; and its exclusive placement in the long opening series to Southampton signals that these "numbers" from 1 to 126 supply the most important chronology of his living record.

Oxford made it possible to measure the time line of the Fair Youth series, because its dynamics dictate that it must conclude when Time runs out upon Elizabeth's death. He was well aware that the date itself, marking the end of forty-five years of extraordinary rule as both a female and an absolute monarch, would become an eternal landmark on the calendar of English and world history.

Queen Elizabeth I died on March 24, 1603, and within hours James of Scotland was proclaimed King James I of England. The Queen's funeral on April 28, 1603, marked the official end of the 118-year Tudor Dynasty.

Funeral: Sonnet 125

"No monarch was officially dead until the day of burial when the great officers of state broke their white wands of office and hurled them into the grave," the British culture expert Roy Strong writes. "So for over a month the old Queen's court went on, as though she were not dead but walking, as she was wont to in the early springtime, in the alleys of her gardens. At last, on 28 April, a funeral procession of some fifteen hundred persons made its way to Westminster Abbey…"

47

Since Oxford lived until June 24, 1604, he had up to fourteen months to revise the sonnets and finish constructing the monument according to those events. Here is the critical moment when the language of Oxford's "invention" converts the "numbers" of the monument into a genuine historical document: given that Southampton failed to succeed Elizabeth, the "time" or real-life time line of the diary must continue beyond her death to the royal funeral procession, when a group of noblemen bore "the canopy" over her effigy and coffin; and we can predict that Oxford would mark this final event with Sonnet 125, which he does:

> Were't ought to me I bore the canopy,
> With my extern the outward honoring,
> Or laid great bases for eternity,
> Which proves more short than waste or ruining?
> Sonnet 125

The living record of Southampton and his royal blood concludes on this solemn occasion, when the Tudor dynasty ceased to exist, followed by Sonnet 126 as the final envoy to "My Lovely Boy."

Liberation: Sonnet 107

Starting at the chronological end and moving backward down the time line, we find the climactic moment of the Fair Youth series at Sonnet 107, known as the "dating" verse because of its obvious topical allusions to the momentous political events in the spring of 1603.

Sonnet 107 celebrates the liberation of Southampton by King James on April 10, 1603 from the Tower of London (a point on which most scholars now agree), after having been imprisoned there for twenty-six months since the Essex Rebellion of February 8,

1601, for which he was convicted of high treason and "supposed as forfeit to a confined doom" in the royal fortress:

> Not mine own fears nor the prophetic soul
> Of the wide world dreaming on things to come
> Can yet the lease of my true love control,
> Supposed as forfeit to a confined doom.
>> Sonnet 107

He gained his freedom precisely because the Queen, known as Cynthia or Diana, goddess of the Moon, has succumbed to her mortality although her eternal self, as a divinely ordained monarch, will endure.

Those who predicted civil war are mocked by their own inaccurate forecasts; now the nobility will crown James amid domestic peace symbolized by olive branches strewn along his route to London and the throne:

> The mortal Moon hath her eclipse endured,
> And the sad Augurs mock their own presage,
> Incertainties now crown themselves assured,
> And peace proclaims Olives of endless age.
>> Sonnet 107

"My love looks fresh," Oxford continues, indicating he may have personally greeted his royal son upon his emergence from the Tower. Continuing in this triumphant mood, he concludes by addressing him directly and referring to the Queen as a "tyrant" whose body will be laid temporarily near the great brass tomb of Henry VII in the Abbey:

And thou in this shalt find thy monument,
When tyrants' crests and tombs of brass are spent.
    Sonnet 107

Final Days: Sonnet 107-126

The nineteen days from Southampton's liberation to Elizabeth's funeral are matched by the nineteen verses from Sonnet 107 to Sonnet 125, one for each day, followed by Sonnet 126 as the "envoy."

These increasingly intense and spiritual verses accompany a solemn march to the procession that will carry the Queen's effigy atop her coffin. These are the final days of the Tudor dynasty, with King James respectfully waiting until after the funeral to enter London and claim the throne.

Prison Years: Sonnets 27-106

The preceding eighty verses (Sonnets 27-106) are most often assigned to the earlier decade of the 1590s, but they have appeared to lack any coherent story. In effect, scholars have faced an "eighty-sonnet gap" in terms of an ability to link these verses to a biographical or historical reality. Now it can be seen, however, that Sonnets 27-106 record events during Southampton's confinement from 1601 to 1603 in the Tower of London.

The most immediate meaning of this context is that, contrary to what has been generally believed, Shakespeare did not at all abandon his beloved Fair Youth while he languished in prison as a convicted traitor. In fact Edward de Vere labored all during that bleak period to produce not only the most intensely sustained poetical sequence the world has known, but, more importantly, to do what he could for Henry Wriothesley in his darkest hour.

This eighty-sonnet sequence rises from the depths of shame and disgrace suffered by Southampton under Elizabeth's contemptuous frown, with Oxford straining to use all his power as an artist to keep shining his light into this darkness:

His beauty shall in these black lines be seen,
And they shall live, and he in them still green.
    Sonnet 63

That in black ink my love may still shine bright.
    Sonnet 65

The eighty prison sonnets are the equivalent of eighty entries of a diary recording "this written ambassage" to a prince in the Tower.

They begin with Sonnet 27 on the night of February 8, 1601, after the Essex Rebellion had failed and Southampton had been taken around midnight through Traitor's Gate. We can only imagine how Oxford had reacted to the tumultuous events of the day, but it is clear even to a casual reader that there is a marked change of mood commencing suddenly at Sonnet 27.

Now, trying to gain some rest in the darkness of his own room, Edward de Vere tells his royal son that "my soul's imaginary sight presents thy shadow to my sightless view, which like a jewel (hung in ghastly night) makes black night beauteous and her old face new," adding, "Lo thus by day my limbs, by night my mind, for thee, and for myself, no quiet find."

This marks the introduction of "shadow" and "black" into the Sonnets, one of the means by which Oxford points to Sonnet 27 as the start of the prison years. The terrible darkness continues for twenty-six months until Southampton's last night in the Tower on April 9, 1603, when Oxford describes the entire prison section in Sonnet 106 as "the Chronicle of wasted time."

Elizabeth died while her son remained in confinement; the

"time" of the chronicle has been "wasted" because the succession took place without him.

The eighty-sonnet prison sequence (27-106) obviously spans more time than Sonnets 107-126, but in fact the first sixty verses (27-86) correspond with events on a day-to-day basis from February 8 to April 8, 1601, when Oxford pointedly marks the end of the daily sonnets by addressing Southampton: "Farewell!"

Then he continues with one sonnet per month until Sonnet 97, which refers to "the fleeting year" (a slang term echoing the Fleet Prison and suggesting "the year of imprisonment") to mark the first anniversary of the Rebellion on February 8, 1602. Afterward the time between sonnets grows longer, as Oxford indicates in several places, such as:

Where art thou, Muse, that thou forget'st so long
To speak of that which gives thee all thy might?
　　Sonnet 100

O truant Muse, what shall be thy amends
For thy neglect of truth in beauty dyed
　　Sonnet 101

He expresses a growing weariness, in parallel with the dwindling life of the Queen:

My love is strengthened, though more weak in seeming...
　　Sonnet 102

Alack what poverty my Muse brings forth...
　　Sonnet 103

Three Winters

Then he reaches Sonnet 104, which refers to "three winters"

(February 1601, February 1602 and February 1603) to mark the second anniversary of the Rebellion on February 8, 1603. After that are two more verses, Sonnets 105 and 106, marking the death of Elizabeth on March 24, 1603 and concluding upon Southampton's final night in the Tower on April 9, 1603.

Scaffolding

If the 100-sonnet center (27-126) had come down to us all by itself, without the other verses that surround it, the historical context of Southampton's confinement in the Tower would have been recognized long before now; but flanking the all-important central sequence are the two segments of twenty-six sonnets apiece, which serve as scaffolding for the full monument:

SONNETS 1-26 mark Southampton's birthdays during his "golden time" of royal hope from age 1 in 1575 to age twenty-six in 1600. The first seventeen coincide with the marriage proposal during 1590-1591 and represent his first seventeen years; the next nine cover the ensuing nine years from 1592 to 1600, the year preceding the Rebellion of February 8, 1601.

These numbers are part of the womb that is recreating Southampton's life.

SONNETS 127-152 make up the Dark Lady series, which Oxford carefully arranged with twenty-six verses to counterbalance the first sequence. He revised two verses from *The Passionate Pilgrim* of 1599 for inclusion here as Sonnets 138 and 144. He focuses on Elizabeth, often addressing her directly in regard to their son, all during the prison years. The series begins with the tragedy of the Rebellion on February 8, 1601 and ends upon her death on March 24, 1603, concluding with the bitter lines of Sonnet 152: "And all my honest faith in thee is lost."

The much-shorter Dark Lady series thus runs in parallel with the Fair Youth Prison Years, though it is composed of fewer verses.

The real-life context of the 100-sonnet center has been hiding in plain sight within the monument. The key to seeing it is our own perception. Now the verses shed light on the history and the history, in turn, illuminates the verses. Neither the official record of events on the calendar nor the consecutive numbering of the verses needs to be rearranged; these two fixed documents, brought into alignment, produce the record that "Shakespeare" left behind for readers in the future:

Not marble nor the gilded monuments
Of Princes shall outlive this powerful rhyme,
But you shall shine more bright in its contents
Than unswept stone, besmeared with sluttish time...
'Gainst death and all oblivious enmity
Shall you pace forth! Your praise shall still find room
Even in the eyes of all posterity
That wear this world out to the ending doom.
 Sonnet 55

Chapter Four

A TUDOR PRINCE

Most of those who conclude that Oxford was the great poet-dramatist agree that the Sonnets hold the answer to the question of Shakespearean authorship, if only we can correctly interpret the poems; but argument over interpretation has continued to divide us. Given an assumption that the Sonnets comprise an autobiographical diary, was Oxford recording a homosexual love affair with young Southampton? Or was he writing to his royal son by the Queen? It would be difficult to find two more extremely different views about a single string of poems.

Or could he have been writing in the Sonnets about an entirely different relationship, one that still eludes our grasp?

My version of the so-called Prince Tudor theory, envisioning Southampton as Oxford's son by the Queen, begins with the fact that her father, Henry VIII, was obsessed about producing a legitimate male heir, to the point that he executed Elizabeth's mother, Anne Boleyn, and broke with the Church of Rome to begin the Protestant Reformation of England. Ascending to the throne in 1558 at twenty-five, Elizabeth projected herself as every inch her father's daughter carrying "the heart and stomach of a king," so it's difficult to believe she would abandon her responsibility to perpetuate the Tudor dynasty.

There's evidence that she had given birth during the 1560s to at least one (and probably more than one) child by Robert Dudley, Earl of Leicester. When Parliament passed an Act in 1571 excluding all but "the natural issue of Her Majesty's body" from succession (significantly emending the term "legal issue" to "natural issue"), it was widely assumed that this new law would allow a royal bastard by Leicester to be put on the throne.

One of those bastards may have been born in 1561 or 1562. The year before Spain's invasion of England by armada in 1588, a twenty-six-year-old man calling himself Arthur Dudley appeared in Madrid claiming to be Leicester's son by Elizabeth; he gave a detailed, persuasive account of his life that could not be disproved.

Sir Francis Englefield, an English Catholic who had gone to work for King Philip, recommended that Spain should hold onto him precisely because the 1571 law stipulated that any "natural issue" of Queen Elizabeth had a royal claim. If such contemporary individuals felt it was possible for her to have unacknowledged heirs, can we rule out that possibility centuries later?

Under constant pressure to find a husband and produce an English successor, Elizabeth was acutely aware of her value as an unmarried female. But she was not Mother Teresa. She continued to hold out the possibility of marriage and to use her femininity for political purposes. The radiant Queen flirted with her courtiers and even openly fondled them, giving Catholic enemies much ammunition to portray her as a whore.

A continuing threat to Elizabeth's life and rule came from Mary Stuart, Queen of Scots, who gave birth to a son, James, in 1566. Two years later, when she began her long captivity on English soil, Mary became a rallying point for those hoping to overthrow the daughter of Henry VIII and restore the Catholic religion. Then came the rising in 1569-70 of the northern Catholic earls, who sought to remove Elizabeth and put Mary on the throne, with the Pope excommunicating the Protestant Queen and declaring that God had sanctioned her murder.

Edward de Vere came to Court in 1571, at age twenty-one, when Elizabeth was thirty-seven and unmarried. Later that year he entered into an arranged family alliance with William Cecil, Lord Burghley, by marrying his fifteen-year-old daughter, Anne Cecil, but quickly rose at Court in the highest personal favor of the Queen, to the point it became Palace gossip that they were as lovers.

Mary Stuart continued to claim the right of succession, while in Scotland her five-year-old son was also a potential English monarch by virtue of his lineage. As threats around the throne continued to build, and now that Queen Elizabeth's love affair with Leicester had ended, she allowed serious negotiations with France for a marriage alliance. This might protect England from Spain's wrath or at least slow down Philip's declaration of outright war.

Massacre

In August 1572, however, while Oxford was with the Queen on the royal progress, word of the St. Bartholomew's Day Massacre in France came as a thunderbolt. Thousands of Protestants had been slain in Paris and the slaughter had spread quickly to the French countryside. Elizabeth and Burghley feared the worst. The same could happen on English soil; their personal lives were in danger as well. Now it was clearer than ever to them that the Protestant Reformation had to move forward; the nation needed its own self-image and unity, not to mention naval power to resist invasion.

The St. Bartholomew's Day Massacre was an Elizabethan wake-up call. In response, Burghley enlisted Francis Walsingham to create a vast intelligence network of spies; and Edward de Vere, working with both men in Her Majesty's service, went on to gather and lead a network of writers (some functioning as agents) to create England's renaissance of literature and drama, giving citizens a new sense of their national history and identity.

Negotiations for the French Match abruptly broke down, but Elizabeth knew they would have to be resumed. Next time, however, she would become a grand actress on the world stage, convincing both France and Spain she would marry the Duke of Alencon, a practicing Catholic who was also nineteen years her junior. It was pure fiction, but Elizabeth would play her part so convincingly that many Puritan subjects, believing it was real, would threaten their own rebellion against the crown.

Against this backdrop of fact and political reality, there existed a window of time during 1573 and 1574 in which Queen Elizabeth, at forty, still had the chance to produce a successor whom she could eventually acknowledge. She was the last of the Tudor line, which would end at her death if no heir existed, so the pressure on her to fulfill this personal and regal responsibility was enormous.

It was reported in May 1573 that Elizabeth was so taken with Edward de Vere that she "delighteth more in his personage and his dancing and his valiantness than any other," while his Puritanical father-in-law, Burghley, "winketh at all these love matters and will not meddle in any way." Such gossip at Court was the result of calculated public relations.

"That Oxford and Elizabeth were lovers can scarcely be doubted," Charlton Ogburn Jr. wrote in 1995, but their act of sexual intercourse would not have been motivated primarily (if at all) by romantic passion; rather, it would have been a political act, calculated to give Elizabeth the means of keeping her options open in the future, when she could point back to the years 1572-1574 and confirm her affair with Oxford.

Could she have kept a pregnancy secret?

Secrecy

The Queen was an absolute monarch, dictating the terms of her public appearances as well as her meetings with Councilors and foreign dignitaries or ambassadors who came to call. She chose her dress of the day from an assortment of styles, many perfect for concealment; entering the room before the guests, she determined the physical setting for any encounter, including how near the visitor could approach.

Other than Lord Burghley (and probably Leicester), only her most intimate Ladies who waited upon her needed to know any such royal secret; if they were inclined to talk, it would be at their peril. A servant entrusted with such sensitive information was by definition an insider within the highest level of the social hierarchy, not to mention physically separated from the public by vast estates and closely guarded palace walls.

Censorship

Elizabeth was the "anointed" and "ordained" head of a totalitarian state run with strict censorship backed by swift punishment for speaking or writing out of turn. There was no "media" in the sixteenth century (as there was when Franklin Delano Roosevelt and John Fitzgerald Kennedy occupied the White House, in the twentieth century, though they still kept personal secrets from the public); printing presses were legally limited and subject to registration; their outputs were scrutinized before publication. The authorities had spies everywhere, watching and listening for sedition; it was an act of treason to spread any rumors about a successor.

Her Majesty's Body

Was she physically capable of bearing children? Burghley wrote long memos about the French Match in 1579, when Elizabeth was in her forty-sixth year, detailing how she was still "very apt for procreation of children," leading his biographer, Conyers Read, to conclude:

"Burghley's discussion of Elizabeth's fruitfulness is the best thing we have on the subject. Coming from him, who was probably better informed than anyone else, and taken in connection with his persistent efforts to get her married in order that she might have children, it comes near to settling the perennial question of her ability to bear children. Certainly it should weigh heavily in the balance against Ben Jonson's idle chatter and the gossip of foreign ambassadors."

Betrothal

Oxford accompanied Elizabeth on a visit to the Archbishop of Canterbury in March 1574, when she would have been five or six months pregnant and they may have been betrothed. Having refused to consummate his marriage to Burghley's daughter, Oxford could have gotten it annulled; and later, if circumstances permitted, Elizabeth could announce she had concealed the fact of their child to play out the French Match, buying time to build up naval strength against Spain's armada. With the support of Burghley, who controlled the nobility and government, such a strategy might well prevail.

Changeling

If Elizabeth gave birth to Oxford's son in late May or early June 1574, the child would have been given to a wet nurse for twelve to eighteen months and also entrusted to another family to be raised as its own. But why place a Tudor prince with the Second Earl of Southampton, a Catholic suspect-traitor she had imprisoned for supporting the northern earls in England who had tried to over-throw her?

In fact no solution could have been better, since the Second Earl had been under the government's close supervision ever since his release from the Tower in May 1573, after a confinement of eight-een months. The official birth date of Henry Wriothesley is October 6, 1573, when the Second Earl wrote a letter (to William More, whom the Privy Council under Lord Burghley had assigned his custody) and reported his wife had given birth that day to a "goodly boy." The evidence suggests the Council had never allowed him conjugal visits in the Tower, so the child (born just five months after his release) was most likely not his, setting up the perfect circumstances for the royal son to be put in place of him as a "changeling boy" in the next year or so.

The Second Earl and his Countess would have been blackmailed. The Queen had the power to send him back to prison or even execute him for treason; she could charge his wife with adultery; and as the subsequent events show, the Southampton household soon became a living hell.

Just as the Queen embarked on progress in July 1574 to the west, and after Oxford had argued with her behind closed doors, he fled without permission to the Continent. If we could have predicted his behavior following the birth of a royal son he could not acknowledge, it would be hard to invent a more emotionally logical reaction.

Literature as History

It goes without saying that documentation of Elizabeth's disposal of a newly born prince before going on progress cannot be expected to appear in the official record.

Where it might well be expected to appear, however, is in the literature of the time – in poetry created precisely to preserve the truth of contemporary royal history in the guise of fiction.

And it would seem that Oxford recorded the story of 1574 in Sonnet 33, by describing the rise of the sun-king with his "sovereign eye" and "golden face" before he was abruptly eclipsed:

> Anon permit the basest clouds to ride
> With ugly rack on his celestial face,
> And from the forlorn world his visage hide,
> Stealing unseen to west with this disgrace.
> Sonnet 33

Setting forth toward Bristol in the west, Elizabeth would have carried her "disgrace" of the boy while giving no outward sign that anything out of the ordinary had happened.

But Oxford recalled his own reaction as the proud father of a royal son, having possession of him for just "one hour" until the "region cloud" (Elizabeth Regina's frown) "masked" him from his sight:

> Even so my Sunne one early morn did shine,
> With all triumphant splendor on my brow,
> But out alack, he was but one hour mine,
> The region cloud hath masked him from me now.
>   Sonnet 33

These lines are insistently personal: my Sunne reflected its golden light on my brow, but he was just one hour mine before Regina's frown masked him from me, then as now; and in the final couplet, he writes that the "stain" (of bastardy) is upon "suns of the world" (princes of England) or "heaven's sun" (Elizabeth's royal son):

> Yet him for this my love no whit disdaineth:
> Suns of the world may stain when heaven's sun staineth.
>   Sonnet 33

Bath

Oxford returned to England three weeks later and caught up to the progress in the west, rejoining Elizabeth (without reprimand) as she and her royal entourage moved to Bristol and then to the ancient Roman city of Bath with its shrines for the curative mineral waters of its hot springs.

In 1780 the Shakespeare editor George Steevens suggested Bath as the setting for Sonnets 153-154; and Sir Greenwood added in

1908 that the "fairest votary" of Sonnet 154 can refer only to Queen
Elizabeth (the "imperial votaress" of *A Midsummer Night's Dream*);
and therefore "Shakespeare" must have accompanied Her Majesty
to the City of Bath.

But the only royal visit to Bath of the entire reign was this one in
August 1574, when Oxford stayed there with the Queen and her
Court for three days. Their son, now a few months old, would have
been with a governess-servant; and as the Bath Sonnets testify,
Edward de Vere would have gone there as "a sad distempered guest"
in desperate need of a "sovereign cure" for his grief that "the boy" or
"the little Love-God" had been "by a Virgin hand disarmed."

The newly born prince, Cupid, derives his "love-kindling fire"
(royal blood) from his mother Elizabeth, the sovereign "mistress" of
England, whose imperial "eye" or viewpoint makes all the difference
in terms of his status, from the beginning:

> But found no cure: the bath for my help lies
> Where Cupid found new fire, my mistress' eye.
> Sonnet 153

Before leaving England in early 1575 on an authorized tour of
France, Germany and Italy, Oxford assured Her Majesty that his
marriage had not been consummated and swore that, if Anne
became pregnant, any such child would not be his. In September he
was in Venice and learned his wife had given birth to a girl, named
Elizabeth Vere (so named in honor of the Queen).

Is it possible that Burghley, fearing Oxford would annul the marriage to Anne, had seen to it that his daughter became pregnant?
Such may be the implication of Hamlet's remark to Polonius, father
of Ophelia:

"Conception is a blessing, but not as your daughter may con-
ceive. Friend, look to't."

Oxford returned to England in April 1576, angrily separating himself from Anne Cecil and the infant girl for the next five years.

Into the Southampton household came a stranger, Thomas Dymocke, who assumed full control of the Second Earl's life. Dymocke prompted him to accuse his wife of adultery; she was sent to another of the earl's residences, put under close surveillance and allowed to receive only limited company there. The Countess would never again live with the boy "Henry Wriothesley" under the same roof, if in fact she ever did.

The charade of the French Match had nearly run its course in 1581, with Alencon making one last try for Elizabeth's hand that year, when a Maid of Honor, Anne Vavasour, gave birth in the Palace to an illegitimate son by Oxford. (Here is an example, ironically enough, of how a pregnancy could be kept secret.)

A Political Deal

Under the Queen's stinging wrath and temporarily banished from her presence, Oxford began discussions with Burghley about reuniting with his wife and trying to beget an heir to his earldom – a dear priority for William Cecil on behalf of his daughter. So began what appears to have been a political deal between Edward de Vere and his father-in-law William Cecil.

Oxford's conditions for returning to Anne Cecil may have included removing his royal son from the Southampton household, so he could begin to forge a bond with the boy (and perhaps use him in his children's acting company). The situation appears to be reflected by Oberon's plea in *A Midsummer Night's Dream* to Queen Titania, who has been universally identified as Queen Elizabeth:

"Why should Titania cross her Oberon? I do but beg a little changeling boy to be my henchman!"

The Second Earl of Southampton was arrested again (on unknown charges) in 1581 and returned to the Tower of London, where he may have been tortured on the rack (or given poison) until his early death was assured. Upon his release, the earl suffered from continually worsening health until he died in October 1581; and in December, just as Edward de Vere and Anne Cecil reunited under the same roof, seven-year-old Henry Wriothesley, Third Earl of Southampton, entered Cecil House as a royal ward of the Queen, who was now his legal mother.

"I then did ask of her her changeling child," Oberon says, "which straight she gave me; and her fairy sent to bear him to my bowre in fairy land. And now I have the boy, I will undo this hateful imperfection of her eyes."

Oxford's negotiations in 1581 with Burghley also must have included plans for Southampton to eventually marry Elizabeth Vere (and beget an heir to consummate the union), in which case the chief minister would support the young earl's royal claim. If and when Henry Wriothesley ascended as King Henry IX, his wife, Burghley's granddaughter, would be Queen — instantly raising the Cecils to the status of royalty.

Could such a plan succeed? Lord Treasurer Burghley was the most powerful man in England, upon whom Elizabeth had become increasingly dependent. If anyone could arrange for the royal succession, either during her life or upon her death, it was he.

War

The Earl of Sussex, patron of the company presenting Oxford's "comedies" at Court, died in 1583; but spymaster Walsingham promptly instigated a new group, the Queen's Men. As wartime efforts increased, the writers under Oxford's guidance and support kept turning out English history plays to rouse patriotic unity.

The Anglo-Spanish War became official in 1584, as England continued to build its naval defense. In mid-1586, the Queen signed an extraordinary Privy Seal warrant granting Oxford an annual thousand pounds (with no accounting needed) from the same source used to dispense Secret Service funds, no doubt paying him for past and future expenditures involving writers and actors.

Burghley masterminded Elizabeth's execution of Mary Stuart in early 1587, ensuring the Spanish invasion; and the defeat of King Philip's Armada in 1588 marked a turning point in the Queen's reign after three decades of rule. At the time, however, few predicted she would continue to live for nearly fifteen more years.

Chapter Five

THE EARL OF SOUTHAMPTON

In October 1589, when Henry Wriothesley officially turned sixteen, Burghley began to pressure him into hurriedly marrying his granddaughter, fourteen-year-old Lady Elizabeth Vere. Southampton stalled, asking for a year to ponder entering a Cecil alliance, as Oxford had done a generation earlier; and when the year was up and his answer was still negative, the Queen and Burghley turned up the pressure, even visiting the Southampton estates in the summer of 1591.

Meanwhile the poet to become known a few years later as "Shakespeare" was completing seventeen private verses to the seventeen-year-old lord, accusing him of committing "murderous shame" and "murderous hate" and calling him a "beauteous niggard" and a "profitless usurer" for stubbornly refusing.

Oxford was not only urging but also commanding his son to beget an heir, in order to guarantee the chief minister's eventual support for his royal claim; this is the most plausible explanation for the urgent tone of these sonnets. The deal with Burghley was the only practical chance for Southampton to succeed Elizabeth, but it would remain in active play for a limited time. The author's personal concern in the Sonnets about Southampton's "roof" and "house" suddenly becomes understandable, for the first time, from the perspective that Oxford is talking about the House of Tudor itself – which now depends on Henry Wriothesley alone for its continuance and which, by his stubbornness, is being allowed to collapse:

> Seeking that beauteous roof to ruinate,
> Which to repair should be thy chief desire.
>> Sonnet 10

Who lets so fair a house fall to decay…
  Sonnet 13

"It is indeed hard to think of any real situation in which it would be natural," C. S. Lewis remarks about the marriage-and-propagation sonnets. "What man in the whole world, except a father or a potential father-in-law, cares whether any other man gets married?"

"Make thee another self for love of me," Oxford pleads in Sonnet 10, with an urgent concern for the perpetuation of Southampton's bloodline that was far more logically the plea of a father.

"Though Southampton persisted to the end in his refusal to marry Lady Elizabeth Vere," biographer Akrigg writes, "it was not for want of urging of marriage by William Shakespeare."

Southampton spurned the older generation's arrangements. He was looking to free himself from his existence as a ward and make his entrance at Court, confident he would rise in the highest royal favor of his mother, the Queen. So why should he choose (as his father, Oxford, had done) to remain under William Cecil's domination?

Elizabeth and Burghley dropped their pressure for the arranged marriage in the fall of 1591.

"Shakespeare"

Anne Cecil had died in June 1588; and now in late 1591, at age forty-one, Edward de Vere quietly remarried, withdrawing from Court and the public eye (undoubtedly to make way for his royal son, and to avoid having to be seen with him). His new wife was Elizabeth Trentham, a Maid of Honor to the Queen, who normally punished any courtier who dared to marry one of her ladies, but this time adopted a gracious attitude.

The new Countess gave birth to Edward de Vere's first surviving son, the future Eighteenth Earl of Oxford, on February 24, 1593.

The boy was christened on March 31, 1593, and given the name Henry de Vere, the first Henry in either parent's lineage.

Less than three weeks later, on April 18, 1593, the sophisticated narrative poem *Venus and Adonis* was registered for publication with the dedication by William Shakespeare of this "first heir of my invention" to Henry Wriothesley, Third Earl of Southampton.

The end game of political struggle, aimed at controlling the royal succession, had publicly begun with the death of spymaster Francis Walsingham in 1590. William Cecil, Lord Treasurer Burghley was already grooming his little hunchbacked son, the cunning Robert Cecil, to fill the spymaster's post as Principal Secretary and eventually continue the Cecilian power behind the throne; but rising in opposition was another royal ward, several years older than Southampton, who had become a military hero and Elizabeth's newest Court favorite: the tall, handsome, swashbuckling, brilliant, high-strung Robert Devereux, Second Earl of Essex, whose popularity rivaled that of the monarch herself.

Southampton would take his chances with Essex; when he came of age, he would join his military adventures and, amid public acclaim, the two popular earls would eclipse the power of the Cecils to create England's policies and determine the nation's future.

Regardless of his disappointment over his royal son's decision to take matters into his own hands, Oxford would have given himself no other choice but to support him. Withdrawing from sight, he took the fateful step of issuing *Venus and Adonis* of 1593 and *Lucrece* of 1594 with their extraordinary dedications to Southampton as by "William Shakespeare," the name suggesting a mighty poet-warrior shaking the spear of his pen while striding onto the stage of history.

Oxford might as well have publicly proclaimed his paternity in these open letters directly addressing the Earl of Southampton.

Deliberately using the imagery of child-bearing, he wrote of *Venus and Adonis* that:

"… if the first heir of my invention prove deformed, I shall be sorry it had so noble a Godfather, and never after ear so barren a land, for fear it yield me still so bad a harvest."

He concluded by stating that Henry Wriothesley was "the world's hopeful expectation," just as King Henry IV reminds his son, Prince Hal, that he must fulfill "the hope and expectation of thy time."

And in the *Lucrece* dedication, Oxford wrote as a subject vowing eternal servitude and bondage to his King:

"Were my worth greater, my duty would show greater; meantime, as it is, it is bound to your Lordship, to whom I wish long life, still lengthened with all happiness. Your Lordship's in all duty, William Shakespeare."

He was boldly letting Elizabeth and the Court know where he stood and where he expected her and other nobles to stand, regardless of Southampton's defiance of the marriage arrangement. He was also letting the Cecils know which side he was on. Meanwhile he was lifting Henry Wriothesley to the height of popular awareness; from here on, the names Shakespeare and Southampton went together in the public mind.

Behind the scenes in the 1590s, Oxford busily revised many of his earlier plays for the Lord Chamberlain's Men ("Shakespeare's Company") to stage for crowds in the London playhouses. Meanwhile Essex and Southampton were given privileged, private use of his revised plays, such as *Love's Labour's Lost,* to entertain members of their faction. The overriding theme of the history plays is succession of the monarch and the question of who should wear the crown.

Oxford could not allow "Shakespeare" to appear on publications of plays until Burghley died at seventy-eight in 1598. By then Robert Cecil had officially held the post of Principal Secretary for two years, so the transfer of bureaucratic control from father to son was unchallenged.

Now, however, there appeared *Palladis Tamia,* a book of commonplace observations by Francis Meres with an inserted announcement that "Shakespeare," the poet, was also the great dramatist who had written plays that had already been performed on stage. These included *The Two Gentlemen of Verona, The Comedy of Errors, Love's Labour's Lost, A Midsummer Night's Dream, The Merchant of Venice, Richard II, Richard III, Henry IV, King John, Titus Andronicus* and *Romeo and Juliet.*

As if taking their cue, London printers began issuing texts of plays by "Shakespeare" or "Shake-speare" by the fall of 1598; and it would seem, in retrospect, that Oxford himself had written Meres's inserted announcement.

Meres also cites Oxford in the same work (as among those "best for comedy"), which, of course, has led orthodox scholars to conclude (or argue) that Shakespeare and Oxford must have been two different persons.

The year before, Southampton had joined Essex on the "Islands Voyage" in pursuit of Spanish treasure ships, a venture that had failed despite Wriothesley's show of bravery and leadership. Stung by Elizabeth's criticism, and goaded into a trap by Secretary Cecil's politic maneuvering, Essex agreed to become the Queen's General of an army against the rebellion in Ireland. He and Southampton left in March 1599 with 15,000 soldiers; and soon crowds at the play house heard "Shakespeare" express support through lines inserted for the chorus of *Henry V:*

Were now the General of our gracious Empress,
As in good time he may, from Ireland coming,
Bringing rebellion broached on his sword,
How many would the peaceful city quit to welcome him!

The Irish campaign was a disaster, with Essex disobeying orders by agreeing to a truce with the Earl of Tyrone, leader of the rebels. When he and Southampton returned without authorization, the Queen put her General under house arrest and forbade Henry Wriothesley to come into her presence. The clear victor was Cecil, whose whisperings in Elizabeth's ear increasingly dictated her emotions, her attitudes and her policies.

Oxford privately recorded the situation in Sonnet 25, which coincides precisely with 1599 in the year-by-year chronology of Sonnets 1-26. He referred to Southampton and Essex as "Great Princes' favorites," that is, Elizabeth's favorites, who were now in a state of dishonor beneath her monarch's frown:

Great Princes' favorites their fair leaves spread,
But as the Marigold at the sun's eye,
And in themselves their pride lies buried,
For at a frown they in their glory die.
    Sonnet 25

In the fall of 1599, as word of a rising against Cecil began to spread, Southampton and his friend Roger Manners, Fifth Earl of Rutland, went daily to the London playhouses. Their purpose was not recreational or cultural, but political. Seated high behind the stage in full view of the crowds, they openly associated themselves with politically charged plays such as *Julius Caesar* and *King John* as by "Shakespeare," the invisible supporter of Southampton and the dramatist of England's royal history, which mirrored current events. (One of Oxford's brazen depictions was that of himself as Falstaff, the father figure, in relation to Southampton as Prince Hal, who progresses from dissolute heir apparent to the responsible, popular, strong leader and monarch, King Henry V.)

Rebellion

Essex grew increasingly desperate. Elizabeth, turning sixty-seven in September 1600, could die at any moment and leave Cecil to guide the succession and retain his power regardless of who ruled next. In the opening days of February 1601, as supporters continued to filter into London to await instructions, Southampton took charge of planning for a surprise assault on Whitehall Palace to forcibly remove the Secretary from his control and even, if necessary, to murder him.

Members of the Essex faction approached the Chamberlain's Men on February 6, 1601, offering payment for a special performance of *Richard II* at the Globe; and many historians feel Southampton, because of his tie to "Shakespeare," must have sought and gained authority from the dramatist himself to use his play for propaganda.

(Looney found "much evidence" that, during the previous few years, Southampton had been the "intermediary" between Oxford and those staging and publishing the dramas. Six plays attributed to Shakespeare were printed during 1600, but all such "authorized" publications abruptly stopped upon Southampton's imprisonment early the next year. Looney suggested that "the complete issue of the plays had been decided upon and begun," but that Southampton's tragedy because of the failed Rebellion had "interfered" with the plans.)

Oxford undoubtedly wrote the "deposition scene" of *Richard II* in support of the effort by both Essex and Southampton to gain access to Elizabeth. As the Queen would later complain, the play was played "forty times" in private venues for the Essex faction, though its powerful deposition scene would not be published as part of the text until 1608. In the latter part of her reign, Essex became associated with Bolinbroke, who maneuvered Richard into doing what the earls hoped they could persuade Elizabeth to do:

"With mine own hands I give away my crown..."

Cecil later accused Essex of plotting to become King himself, but he was exaggerating the earl's motives to ensure his destruction. So long as Elizabeth relied upon the hunchbacked Secretary, who controlled access to her, Essex and Southampton had no way of being heard.

Rebellion was "a last resort" for Essex, observed G. W. Keeton, Professor of English Law at University College in London, adding, "But there seems no reason to doubt that his real object was to induce the Queen to replace Cecil by himself."

Now the testimony of the Sonnets supports that observation while explaining the Rebellion in a new way. If Essex had taken Cecil's place as head of the Privy Council, it is possible he would have called a Parliament to proclaim Henry Wriothesley, Earl of Southampton as Elizabeth's immediate heir and successor.

Although he remained behind the scenes, Oxford became personally involved in the rising (and in the crime for which the earls were charged) because of the staging of *Richard II* on Saturday, February 7, 1601. The next morning, provoked into precipitous action by Cecil's agents in their midst, Essex and Southampton led 300 armed men in what became known as the Essex Rebellion, resulting in wild chaos, some bloodshed and mass arrests. That night, the two earls knelt and surrendered up their swords to the Crown; then they were taken through Traitors Gate to await trial for high treason.

Trial

Having already found a "vital link" between Oxford and Southampton in regard to the marriage arrangement of 1590-1591, Looney reported an even more important link in terms of the trial of Essex and Southampton on February 19, 1601, when both were found guilty and condemned to death. Here is how he described it:

"In the year 1601 there took place the ill-fated insurrection under the Earl of Essex; an insurrection which its leaders maintained was aimed, not at the throne, but at the politicians, amongst whom Robert Cecil, son of Burghley, was now prominent. Whether Edward de Vere approved of the rising or not, it certainly represented social and political forces with which he was in sympathy...

"In order to stir up London and to influence the public mind in a direction favorable to the overturning of those in authority, the company gave a performance of *Richard II*, the Earl of Southampton subsidizing the players. In the rising itself Southampton took an active part. Upon its collapse he was tried for treason along with its leader Essex; and it was then that Edward de Vere emerged from his retirement for the first time in nine years to take his position amongst the twenty-five peers who constituted the tribunal before whom Essex and Southampton were to be tried.

"It is certainly a most important fact in connection with our argument [of Edward de Vere as the author of Shakespeare's works] that this outstanding action of Oxford's later years should be in connection with the one contemporary that 'Shakespeare' has immortalized...

"It is clear, from the point of view of the problem of Shakespearean authorship, that the famous trial of the Earl of Essex assumes quite a thrilling interest. Standing before the judges was the only living personality that 'Shakespeare' has openly connected with the issue of his works and towards whom he has publicly expressed affection: Henry Wriothesley... and sitting on the benches amongst the judges was none other, we believe, than the real 'Shakespeare' himself..."

Along with the other peers, Oxford had no choice but to support the Crown by voting guilty against both earls and sending them to their deaths. Essex was beheaded six days later, on February 25,

1601, and four other conspirators were executed before people realized that the Queen had apparently decided to spare Southampton.

No public explanation was given and no legal reason was ever recorded. A convicted traitor in shame and disgrace, Southampton was now referred to in documents as "Mr. Henry Wriothesley," a base commoner (or "the late earl," as he was called in the eyes of the law). He was stripped of all his titles and lands and regarded as serving a sentence of perpetual confinement.

Blackmail

Oxford had adopted the Shakespeare name to support Southampton in the struggle to determine control over succession. When the Rebellion failed, the victorious Cecil sent Essex to his execution and then aimed to bring James of Scotland to the throne and thereby retain his own power in the new reign.

The Secretary secured a reprieve for Southampton while holding him hostage in the Tower, under the continuing threat he might still be executed at any moment. This pressurized situation continued for as long as Elizabeth remained alive and until the succession of James was assured.

To save his son's life and secure the promise of his release from the Tower with a pardon, Oxford agreed to renounce all ties to Southampton — as his father and, therefore, as "Shakespeare." Having associated Henry Wriothesley (and him alone) with that name, Oxford was forced to glue the mask to his own face; and Southampton, in turn, had to renounce his royal claim.

Such was the infamous bargain, in the face of blackmail, that Edward de Vere made with Robert Cecil – who desperately needed to bring about a succession without challenge. And because of this sacrifice by both father and son, James of Scotland became King of England and the nation's destiny was forever altered.

Chapter Six

A NEW TIME FRAME

Traditional scholars of the Stratfordian authorship have known the correct Fair Youth of the Sonnets for nearly two centuries, ever since Nathan Drake identified Southampton in 1817. The correct poet of the Sonnets was identified in 1920 by J. Thomas Looney, bringing Oxford and Southampton together in what is perhaps the deepest expression of love and commitment from one man to another in the history of literature.

Anyone reading Oxford's surviving poems and letters under his own name will agree that the voice of the Sonnets certainly could be his; but even those accepting him as their author have lacked the all-important time frame within which to perceive the story as well as the relationship between Oxford and Southampton. Knowing the correct author and the correct younger man is crucial, but the additional element required is the context of time and circumstance within which the real-life drama is being recorded.

Hyder Rollins put it this way in 1944:

"The question when the sonnets were written is in many respects the most important of all the unanswerable questions they pose. If it could be answered definitely and finally, there might be some chance of establishing to general satisfaction the identity of the friend, the dark woman, and the rival (supposing that all were real individuals), of deciding what contemporary sources Shakespeare did or did not use, and even of determining whether the order of Q is the author's or not. In the past and at the present, such a solution has been and remains an idle dream."

Imagine coming upon Hamlet's "To be or not to be" soliloquy without the context of the play in which it appears. In that case, we could not comprehend it in terms of the individuals and events causing the Prince to express such thoughts and emotions. The soliloquy would remain a powerful, universal, timeless expression of the human condition, but we could not use it to learn the specific circumstances of Hamlet's predicament. We could not even discover that in fact the Prince of Denmark was the speaker.

So it has been with the Sonnets, which are the poet's own version of Hamlet's soliloquies, using the personal pronoun "I" to express himself. These verses are equally powerful, universal and timeless, as readers around the world have understood for centuries; but there has been no surrounding context within which to perceive them as part of a real-life historical drama.

The simple answer put forth here, as outlined, is that the first eighty entries of the 100-sonnet center sequence correspond with the twenty-six months of Southampton's confinement in the Tower; and this context of "when" confirms Rollins's prediction that some age-old enigmas about the Sonnets can now be resolved:

Fair Youth

Southampton was indeed the younger man confined in the Tower, so the majority of scholars have been correct in identifying him as the "Fair Youth" of the Sonnets.

Dark Lady

While in prison, Southampton could not have been part of an active "love triangle" with the poet and his mistress. The powerful, deceitful, tyrannical "Dark Lady" who steals him away could only have been Queen Elizabeth, the Sovereign Mistress of England, who was holding him captive in her prison-fortress while casting her imperial dark frown of disgrace upon him.

Rival Poet

No other writers were competing publicly for Southampton's attention or patronage during his bleak time in the Tower, so the "Rival Poet" who makes his appearance in Sonnets 77-86 can only have been the popular name "William Shakespeare," a name with which Henry Wriothesley had already been uniquely associated. In this context the so-called Rival Poet series is a record by Oxford of his personal sacrifice, according to the bargain by which "Shakespeare" must continue to live as a "spirit" while he, Oxford, must be "struck dead" in terms of his identity as the world perceives it:

> Was it his spirit, by spirits taught to write
> Above a mortal pitch, that struck me dead?
> > Sonnet 86

Author

The poet testifies he was summoned to the "Sessions" or treason trial of Essex and Southampton, just as Edward de Vere was the highest-ranking earl summoned to the trial at Westminster Hall on February 19, 1601.

"Thy adverse party is thy Advocate," Oxford promises Southampton in Sonnet 35, recording that he must perform his duty to the state by condemning him to death, but also that he will act as his legal counsel in an attempt to save him.

This radically new perception of the context of time and circumstance brings us to the heart of the authorship mystery and confirms that only Oxford could have been the real "Shakespeare."

Three Winters

Oxford tells Southampton in Sonnet 104 it had been "three Winters ... since first I saw you fresh," which scholars have taken to mean a three-year period during the 1590s. In the context being set forth here, however, Oxford is referring to the three winters from the Earl of Southampton's imprisonment on February 8, 1601, through the subsequent two anniversaries of the Rebellion in February 1602 and February 1603. It is a two-year period encompassing three actual winters.

Darkness

A cloud of emotional darkness descends upon the diary at the start of the 100-verse center, with Sonnet 27, when Oxford envisions Southampton in the Tower as "a jewel hung in ghastly night." Anticipating that his son may soon be executed, he describes him in Sonnet 30 as "precious friends hid in death's dateless night" and in Sonnet 31 as "the grave where buried love doth live."

Disgrace

With the darkness comes a wave of shame and disgrace covering both the poet and the Fair Youth. When Oxford writes in Sonnet 29 that he is "in disgrace with Fortune and men's eyes" (in disgrace with Elizabeth and her subjects), it's not only because he suffers in place of his son, but also because he had deliberately and publicly used the "Shakespeare" name to encourage active opposition to the power of Robert Cecil.

"All men make faults," Oxford tells Southampton, also in Sonnet 35, "and even I in this, authorizing thy trespass with compare." That is, he had been an accessory to the "trespass" or crime that the government chose to call treason, having sanctioned the Rebellion (using the Shakespeare name) by dramatizing ("authorizing") how a weak monarch, King Richard II, had given up his crown; and months later, the still-furious Elizabeth would blurt out: "I am Richard II, know ye not that!"

Legal Language

Now the many legal terms which appear throughout the Sonnets are revealed as related to the crime, the trial, the prison, the legal bargaining for Southampton's life and freedom, the need for a royal pardon, and more:

Accessory, Accusing, Action, Adverse Party, Advocate, Arrest, Attaint, Attainted, Bail, Bars, Blame, Confess, Confine, Commits, Crime, Defendant, Defense, Excuse, False ("false-traitor"), Fault, Faults, Gate, Gates of Steel, Guard, Guilt, Impaneled (a jury), Imprisoned, Judgment, Key, Lawful Plea, Lawful Reasons, Laws, Liberty, Locked Up, Misprision, Offence, Offender, Pardon, Plea, Plea Deny, Plead, Prove, Purposed Overthrow, Quest (jury), Ransom, Releasing, Repent, Revolt, Sessions, Summon, Suspect (suspect-traitor), Term of Life, Trespass, Up-Locked, Verdict, Wards (guards)…

Separation

The grief-stricken poet's "separation" from the Fair Youth has never been explained, but in this context Oxford is expressing his agony that his son is being held hostage in the Tower while facing the threat of execution — a threat Cecil held over him for more than two years, until Elizabeth finally died and the succession of James was assured, leaving the Secretary still in control:

Things Removed, O Absence, Absence of Your Liberty, Absent From Thy Heart, Where Thou Art, Injurious Distance, Where Thou Dost Stay, Removed From Thee, Present-Absent, Where Thou Art, The Bitterness of Absence, Where You May Be, Where You Are, The imprisoned Absence of Your Liberty, Where You List, Thou Dost Wake Elsewhere, All Away, Be Absent From Thy Walks, How Like a Winter Hath My Absence Been From Thee, This Time Removed, Thou Away, You Away…

Relationship

Once Oxford is seen as a mature nobleman writing to another lord a generation younger, the traditional notion of "poet-to-patron" must be eliminated. Furthermore, as Southampton was in the Tower all during that time, they could have been engaged neither in an active homosexual relationship nor in an active, bisexual love triangle with the Dark Lady.

The Sonnets do contain sexual allusions, but the circumstances are that the Queen is holding Southampton in the Tower and that Oxford is furious at his Sovereign Mistress for not helping him. What relationship, other than father-to-royal-son, could have caused fifty-year-old Edward de Vere to feel such painful, agonizing, personal responsibility for Southampton and his fate?

Oxford used the sonnets as a genuine outlet for his grief, expressing the torment of feeling responsible for Southampton's fate. It appears that at times during the prison years, he wrote several entries at a single sitting, before arranging them according to the calendar – confirming the "linkages" between clustered sonnets that scholars have noted.

"But day doth daily draw my sorrows longer," he records in Sonnet 28, compiling his entries day by day, "and night doth nightly make grief's length seem stronger."

"Though thou repent, yet I have still the loss," he tells the Southampton in Sonnet 34, adding, "Th'offender's sorrow lends but weak relief to him that bears the strong offence's loss."

In the most reverent way, as father of a divinely ordained prince, Oxford becomes a Christ figure bearing the guilt and burden of all sins.

"So shall those blots that do with me remain," Oxford promises him in Sonnet 36, "without thy help by me be borne alone."

With Cecil firmly in charge, Oxford knew the price to "ransom" his son's life and freedom would be the loss of Southampton's claim to the throne. Their relationship as father and son must be buried, now and forever.

"I may not ever-more acknowledge thee," he tells Southampton in Sonnet 36, "lest my bewailed guilt should do thee shame. Nor thou with public kindness honor me, unless thou take that honor from thy name."

Oxford writes in Sonnet 37 as a "decrepit father" who "takes delight to see his active child do deeds of youth" and cries out in Sonnet 39 that his son is "all the better part of me," adding, "Even for this, let us divided live, and our dear love lose name of single one."

Elizabeth held Southampton in her prison and could send him to his death: "That she hath thee is of my wailing chief," Oxford moans in Sonnet 42, writing as a father who would be the chief mourner or closest relative at his son's funeral. In this tragic way, mother and son are together at last, as jailer and prisoner:

"Both find each other, and I lose both twain, and both for my sake lay on me this cross."

The forty days and nights from the Rebellion equal the time of Christ's trial in the wilderness. On the fortieth day, March 19, 1601, Oxford records the Queen's decision to spare the life of her son while keeping him a prisoner; and his reaction is one of emotional exhaustion, recorded in a virtual suicide note in Sonnet 66 by enumerating reasons he prefers to die.

Alluding perhaps to Essex, who has by now been executed, and certainly to Southampton, who has been deprived of his royal claim, he writes that the "strength" of such purposeful men has been "by limping sway disabled" – destroyed by the limping, swaying, hunchbacked figure of Secretary Cecil, who now held "sway" or power over his enemies. And concluding his lamentation, Oxford reiterates he would prefer to depart from this world, were it not for the fact it would mean leaving his royal son alone, possibly to die, in the Tower:

Tired with all these, from these would I be gone,
Save that to die, I leave my love alone.
     Sonnet 66

What follows is Oxford's descent into another kind of death. Southampton has eluded the swift blade of the executioner's axe, but Oxford now wonders why his son should be forced to serve a life sentence with "infection," or criminals in the Tower:

Ah, wherefore with infection should he live,
And with his presence grace impiety ...
     Sonnet 67

Southampton will be able to "live a second life on second head," his father writes in Sonnet 68, adding in Sonnet 70: "Thou hast passed by the ambush of young days." But their true relationship will never be seen by the contemporary world, so Oxford is forced to instruct him in Sonnet 71:

"No longer mourn for me when I am dead...Nay, if you read this line, remember not the hand that writ it, for I love you so, that I in your sweet thoughts would be forgot, if thinking on me then should make you woe...Do not so much as my poor name rehearse..."

The litany continues in Sonnet 72:

"After my death, dear love, forget me quite, for you in me can nothing worthy prove...My name be buried where my body is, and live no more to shame nor me nor you. For I am shamed by that which I bring forth," Oxford cries out, referring to himself as a father who brought forth a Prince unable to wear the crown.

Sonnet 73, a funeral dirge, reflects Oxford's writing of *The Phoenix and the Turtle* for publication in this same year of 1601:

"That time of year thou mayst in me behold, when yellow leaves, or none, or few, do hang upon those boughs which shake against the cold, bare ruined choirs, where late the sweet birds sang," he tells Southampton, adding:

"In me thou seest the twilight of such day, as after Sun-set fadeth in the West" — his glorious royal son who is fading, even now, from the world's view.

Behind the scenes, without the Queen becoming aware of it, Oxford must lend his full support to James; and Southampton must remain in the Tower, where he will disappear if this transition of royal power fails to occur.

"O how I faint when I of you do write," Oxford tells his son in Sonnet 80, "knowing a better spirit doth use your name, and in the praise thereof spends all his might to make me tongue-tied speaking of your fame."

The rise of "Shakespeare" as the "better spirit" who has immortalized Southampton means Oxford's simultaneous fall into oblivion:

Your name from hence immortal life shall have,
Though I (once gone) to all the world must die.
    Sonnet 81

These two lines sum up and explain the mystery of the "Shakespeare" authorship that has continued from then to now.

Chapter Seven

A NEW CONTEXT

By the fall of 1998, it seemed that any solution to the Sonnets was beyond reach; but I decided to make one last try before giving up. First I listed a series of hypotheses with one major prediction: If these verses contain a true story for the benefit of "eyes not yet created" (Sonnet 81) in future generations, the poet would have made certain that we would be able to comprehend it.

This time around, I started searching through for any "instructions" he may have inserted. If he had left such a means of reading his words, I would follow it literally; and in the end, this key would have to provide some new and different kind of information. I had no idea what any such discovery might look like, but it needed to be extremely persuasive for me to continue my quest.

In the previous two years, while completing a book about scientific visualization, I had posed this simple, overall question: What if the sonnet sequence of Shakespeare comprised a single masterwork, its various elements of language, design and content operating in harmony as part of the whole?

If such were true, I thought, then some unifying system must exist; and there might be a central mechanism, similar in a general way to the "double helix" structure of DNA, with its consistent vocabulary determining the form and functions of a living organism.

So that's what I started to look for; and in Sonnet 76, at what turns out to be the exact center of the structure of an elegant monument, here was the "invention" (special language) by which Oxford writes about a single subject that is "all one, ever the same" (Southampton and Elizabeth) with "every word" while "dressing old

words new" or exchanging one word for another to consistently signify any given aspect of the same family triangle.

Here, for example, is how he refers to Elizabeth in the Sonnets
not only as "beauty," but, also, how he keeps "varying to other
words" (Sonnet 105) to signify the Queen:

BEAUTY – Venus, goddess of Love and Beauty
DIAN – Diana, goddess of the Moon
FAIREST VOTARY – the "imperial Vot'ress" of A
Midsummer Night's Dream
EVER THE SAME – she translated her motto,
Semper Eadem, into English this way
FORTUNE – she was associated with Fortune
GODDESS – the divinely ordained goddess on earth
HEAVEN – she was associated with Heaven
LADIES DEAD – she was "our sovereign Lady"
MISTRESS – "our Sovereign Mistress"
MOON – Cynthia or Diana, goddess of the Moon
MOTHER – wife and mother of her subjects
NATURE – she was associated with Nature
PHOENIX – she adopted the phoenix as an emblem
PRINCES – she was the Prince of England
REGION – she was Elizabeth Regina
ROSE – her dynasty of the Tudor Rose began in 1485
THRONED QUEEN – Queen on the English throne
VIRGIN HAND – Virgin Queen, vows not to marry
WE – she used the royal "we" on official documents

All these words reverberate with their own particular multiple
meanings, thereby enriching the literary allusions and rhetorical
devices used to convey the subject matter; but in fact each word sig-
nifies the Queen, or some aspect of her Majesty, in relation to the

actual history that Oxford is recording and intending to preserve for posterity.

Within the family triangle, Elizabeth casts the shadow of her frown upon Southampton, so he becomes:

Bare, Barren, Base, Black, Blamed, Dark, Darkly, Dateless, Despised, Disdained, Disgraced, False, Forlorn, Foul, Ghastly, Hidden, Masked, None, Profaned, Rank, Rotten, Sable, Scorned, Shamed, Slandered, Sullen, Sullied, Suspect, Ugly, Unfair, Unseen, Untrimmed, Vulgar, Wasted, Worst...

Oxford shines his light upon him as:

Abundant, Alike, All, Alone, Always, Beauteous, Beloved, Best, Blessed, Bounteous, Bright, Celestial, Clear, Constant, Controlling, Crowned, Darling, Dear, Dearest, Dearly, Divine, Entitled, Eternal, Excellent, Fair, Fairer, Fairest, Fairly, Fragrant, Fresh, Fresher, Full, Gaudy, Gentle, Gentlest, Gently, Gilded, Glorious, Golden, Gracious, Happy, High, Holy, Immortal, Kind, Lovely, Mightier, Near, Nearly, One, Only, Perfect, Powerful, Precious, Proud, Proudly, Pure, Purple, Rare, Religious, Rich, Richer, Right, Rightly, Riper, Scarlet, Silver, Special, Strong, Successive, Sweet, Sweetest, Sweetly, Tall, Tender, True, Virtuous, Wondrous, Worthy...

These are examples of how Edward de Vere, Earl of Oxford keeps "dressing old words new" (Sonnet 76) and "varying to other words" (Sonnet 105) to create diversity within the "noted weed" of poetry while recording the progress of LOVE in relation to TIME, which leads to the time line of the chronicle.

The result is a "double image" created by words: a fictional love story on the surface, while running in parallel is a real-life, treasonous chronicle of royal blood and succession to Elizabeth. The surface story would offer some means of "deniability" if these sonnets got into the wrong hands.

Starting with the hypothesis that Sonnet 107 is recording Southampton's release from the Tower on April 10, 1603, I began to "climb back down the ladder" — numerically, that is — to see, according to Oxford's special language, where he might have begun recording Southampton's imprisonment by marking his entrance into the Tower. Where does he begin to use the "dark" words as well as the legal language? And it came as a complete surprise to me, a shock, to find myself all the way down that ladder to Sonnet 27, where he introduces the words "black" and "shadow" and speaks of Southampton as "like a jewel (hung in ghastly night)." He begins the story of his royal son's imprisonment right here.

And here was an entirely new context for the eighty verses from Sonnet 27 to Sonnet 106. Now I could see that all of them are to and about Southampton during his confinement in the Tower from Sonnet 27 marking February 8, 1601 to Sonnet 106 marking April 9, 1603, his final night as a prisoner.

I believe the numbered verses of the Sonnets are now placed within their chronological framework, one that makes sense for the first time. The pieces all fit together, without need to "imagine" this or that link to the known facts of the history.

In this case, the process has been more similar to placing the verses over the calendar as though they were stencils; the only step then required is to look again at the lines in this light. Time and again, what they say leaps from the page with new meaning and clarity.

Take, for example, Oxford's statement to the Earl of Southampton in Sonnet 42, "That she hath thee is my wailing chief," referring to Elizabeth keeping him in her royal prison fortress. In his edition Stephen Booth glosses "of my wailing chief" as "the principal cause of my wailing," adding:

"The strange and elliptical construction may have been prompted by Shakespeare's wish to echo the already common term 'chief mourner,' the nearest relative present at a funeral."

But that is all he says, because he can offer no context for the poet's insertion of such an echo; but for us the phrase takes on sudden relevance, since we can see that Oxford is now anticipating Southampton's execution and envisioning himself as the father – the nearest relative – at his son's funeral.

Another example is in Sonnet 125, on the occasion of the Queen's funeral procession, when Oxford tells Southampton, "No, let me be obsequious in thy heart." Booth writes that obsequious echoes the procession suggested by the canopy in the first line and the idea of being a follower, adding: "Through its relation to obsequy, 'funeral,' obsequious had the specialized meaning 'dutiful in performing funeral rites,' and invites a reader to think of the canopy as borne in a funeral procession." Once again Booth offers no real-life context, though his statement readily supports and confirms the new timeline, by which Sonnet 125 marks the solemn funeral procession for Elizabeth. One might say it clinches this connection to the contemporary history.

Sonnet 27

"Suddenly we are all adrift, because the spirit of the verses so obviously changes," Gerald Massey wrote in 1866, citing the abrupt transition in both tone and content from Sonnet 26 to Sonnet 27.

Here is what I wrote in *The Monument* at the beginning of the Prison Years:

Oxford is "weary with toil" and finally hastening to bed to rest from his "travail" – not from his "travel" on a physical journey, as some editors have emended it, but from his labors that day and night in reaction to the Rebellion. He lies awake before dawn. "But then begins a journey in my head," he continues, adding that his "thoughts" become purposefully fixed on making "a zealous pilgrimage to thee." His eyes remain wide open in the "darkness" of his sleeping quarters, while "my soul's imaginary sight presents thy shadow to my sightless view." In a dreamlike state while still awake, Oxford finds his son appearing to him as "a jewel hung in ghastly night" — a shining, ghostlike image that "makes black night beauteous and her old face new."

Sonnet 27 presents a vision of Oxford surrounded by physical darkness as he lies in bed and by the emotional darkness of the day's terrible events that have blackened Southampton's honor. Agents of the Crown, rounding up other conspirators that afternoon and evening, have already announced the charges of high treason against the two popular earls. Confined in a room of the Tower in the still-dark hours after midnight, Southampton now appears to Oxford as a bright jewel projected by the inner vision of his soul.

"This is the first of a series of five sonnets in which the poet meditates on his friend." —Katherine Duncan-Jones

The above observation is accurate, except that Sonnet 27 is actually the first of five dozen sonnets that can be seen as corresponding with sixty days from February 8, 1601. Editor Stephen Booth also finds linkages from the outset of this new sequence – from 27 to 28, from 30 to 31 and from 33 to 34, and so on. Such linkages occur throughout the next eighty sonnets, suggesting the Rebellion has triggered Oxford's most intense labor upon the Sonnets and that he is now writing/compiling the equivalent of one per day.

Given such connections, it is easy to imagine him writing two or more sonnets at a time, before arranging them in numerical sequence corresponding to calendar days. It's doubtful that Oxford actually wrote a sonnet each day, but, rather, collected his thoughts before working on clusters or sequences. No doubt all the sonnets were subsequently revised and arranged in their final order after April 1603.

Now it is long past midnight, after the Essex Rebellion has failed, and Southampton is imprisoned in the Tower of London. No more is he "the world's fresh ornament" but, rather, "a jewel hung in

ghastly night." A great darkness has descended over the private verses of the Sonnets; Oxford will write sonnets to correspond with the
day-by-day circumstances as they unfold. His royal son has committed high treason; as a ranking earl, Oxford knows he must sit on
the jury and must find him guilty; as his father, he must also do all
he can to save him from execution.

Already he has begun to "toil" or argue on his son's behalf. Henry
Wriothesley has lost his claim to the throne; and in the darkness at
his Hackney home, Oxford's "thoughts" begin a "journey" or "zealous pilgrimage" to his royal son in the prison:

> Weary with toil, I haste me to my bed,
> The dear repose for limbs with travail tired;
> But then begins a journey in my head
> To work my mind, when body's work's expired.
> For then my thoughts (from far where I abide)
> Intend a zealous pilgrimage to thee,
> And keep my drooping eye-lids open wide,
> Looking on darkness, which the blind do see.
> Save that my soul's imaginary sight
> Presents thy shadow to my sightless view,
> Which like a jewel (hung in ghastly night)
> Makes black night beauteous, and her old face new.
> Lo thus by day my limbs, by night my mind,
> For thee, and for my self, no quiet find.

Sonnet 27 begins the "century" or 100-Sonnet Center of the monument that Oxford will finally construct for Southampton, as a memorial to preserve him and his "love" or royal blood ("And you and love
are still my argument" – Sonnet 76, line 10) for future generations.

Although Southampton and Essex claim they were attempting
only to remove Robert Cecil from his control over the Queen, they
are accused of having committed high treason against the Crown

itself. Essex will die for his sins; Elizabeth will spare the life of her royal son, but his claim of succession has been lost.

One of the great surprises for me has been a much closer link between the Sonnets and the chronicle plays of royal history than most scholars have emphasized. Virtually all adjectives applied to Southampton and his royalty — "precious, sweet, tender, fair, beloved," etc. — are already used in the plays to refer to princes. This also applies to negative words such as "shame" or "disgrace" or "sin", etc, which often appear in Shakespeare's history plays in reference to the same kind of dishonor suffered by Southampton.

After a while it becomes clear that the traditional context of a "love triangle" involving the Poet, the Fair Youth and the Dark Lady is now supplanted by a new context involving matters of the highest political concern, even though such adjectives appear to support both perceptions.

Four particular words of the Sonnets should be mentioned here: "fault", "trespass", "misprision" and "ransom". Traditionally these terms have been seen as metaphors applied to romantic or sexual infidelity; but in the chronicle plays of royal history, they are applied to the same situation faced by Oxford and Southampton because of the Essex Rebellion. "Fault" and "trespass" refer to treason; "misprision" is a lesser form of that crime (Oxford announces in Sonnet 87 that it has been applied to Southampton to save his life and make him eligible for a pardon); "ransom," a term for the fee or payment made by prisoners to gain their release, is what Oxford is paying for his royal son:

> To weigh how once I suffered in your crime...
> But that your trespass now becomes a fee:
> Mine ransoms yours, and yours must ransom me.
> Sonnet 120

Oxford, by means of his painful bargain with Cecil, has ransomed his son from the Tower; and now it will be up to Southampton to "ransom" or liberate Oxford, by making sure the Sonnets are printed for posterity. Edward de Vere has buried the truth of his life from contemporary eyes, but he remains alive in this monument – as he indicates in Sonnet 107: "I'll live in this poor rhyme." Here is a short list of such terms used in the Sonnets and also in Shakespeare's royal history plays:

"Disgrace"

> When in disgrace with Fortune and men's eyes
>> Sonnet 29

> And spit it bleeding in his high disgrace
> *Richard II*, 1.1.194

"Sessions … Summon"

> When to the Sessions of sweet silent thought
> I summon up remembrance of things past
>> Sonnet 30

> Summon a session that we may arraign
> Our most disloyal lady; for, as she hath
> Been publicly accused, so she shall have
> A just and open trial
>> *The Winter's Tale*, 2.3.201-204

"Shame"

> Nor can thy shame give physic to my grief
>> Sonnet 34

> Seize on the shame-faced Henry...
> Hence with him to the Tower
>> *3 Henry VI*, 4.8.52, 57

"Offender ... Ransom"

Th'offender's sorrow lends but weak relief
To him that bears the strong offence's loss.
Ah, but those tears are pearl which thy love sheeds,
And they are rich, and ransom all ill deeds
    Sonnet 34

For I should melt at an offender's tears
And lowly words were ransom for their fault
    2 Henry VI, 3.1.126-127

"Stain"

Clouds and eclipses stain both Moone and Sunne
    Sonnet 35

And that high royalty was ne'er plucked off,
The faiths of men ne'er stained with revolt
    King John, 4.2.5-6

"Fault ... Trespass ... Attainted"

All men make faults, and even I in this,
Authorizing thy trespass with compare
    Sonnet 35

I do confess my fault
And do submit myself to your Highness' mercy
    Henry V, 2.2.77-78

Of faults concealed, wherein I am attainted
    Sonnet 88

And by his treason stand'st thou not attainted,
Corrupted, and exempt from ancient gentry?
His trespass yet lives guilty in thy blood
  1 Henry VI, 2.4.92-94

"Blot"

So shall those blots that do with me remain
  Sonnet 36

And thus thy fall hath a kind of blot
  Henry V, 2.2.138

"Revolt"

Since that my life on thy revolt doth lie…
  Sonnet 93

I will weep for thee,
For this revolt of thine, methinks, is like
Another fall of man
  Henry V, 2.2.140-142

"Purposed Overthrow"

To linger out a purposed overthrow
  Sonnet 90

And you did swear that oath at Doncaster,
That you did nothing purpose 'gainst the state
  1 Henry IV, 5.1.4.42-43

Edward will always bear himself a king.
Though Fortune's malice overthrow my state…
  3 Henry VI, 4.3.45-46

"Pardon"

> O let me suffer, being at your beck,
> Th'mprisoned absence of your liberty...
> To you it doth belong
> Your self to pardon of self-doing crime
> > Sonnet 58

> Say 'pardon,' king, let pity teach thee how;
> The word is short, but no so short as sweet;
> No word like 'pardon' for kings' mouths so meet
> > *Richard II*, 5.3.114-116

"Ambush"

> Thou hast passed by the ambush of young days
> > Sonnet 70

> Once did I lay an ambush for you life,
> A trespass that doth vex my grieved soul
> > *Richard II,* 1.1.137-138

"Misprision"

> The charter of thy worth gives thee releasing...
> So thy great gift, upon misprision growing,
> Comes home again, on better judgment making
> > Sonnet 87

> Either envy, therefore, or misprision
> Is guilty of this fault, and not my son
> > *1 Henry IV*, 1.3.26-27

Such words are woven within the "noted weed" or fabric of the familiar poetry so that they, too, have been hiding in plain sight.

Darkness

One way of recognizing the eighty verses from Sonnet 27 to Sonnet 106 of the "prison years" is by the fact that most of the "dark" words are found here. The following words are used exclusively in this section:

Black (9 times); Base (5); Blot (4); Canker (5); Cloud (3); Dark/Darkness (4); Guilt (1); Scorn (2); Shade & Shadow (6); Sin/Sins (5); Stain (3)

Other such words appear almost exclusively during the prison years:

Crime (3); Death (12); Disgrace (6); Hate (8); Night & Nightly (14); Shame (7)

To rephrase my description of a discovery:

When I first thumbed backward down the sequence from Sonnet 107, I began to follow these "dark" words and was surprised to realize that their onslaught begins all the way back in Sonnet 27, where "black" and "shadow" make their first appearance. Only afterward came the process of laying out the sonnets side by side with the actual dates of recorded events; and it was then, moving forward again with the Elizabethan calendar, I realized that the tragic events of 1601-03 comprise the heart of the Sonnets.

Royal Words

In his dynastic diary Oxford uses direct and obvious terms related to royalty, such as:

Canopy, crown, crowned, god, king, kings, kingly, kingdom, kingdoms, queen, majesty, monarch, politic, policy, princes, reign, sovereign, state, succession, successive.

But these are only the more "direct" or specifically royal words. Some of the others, perhaps less obvious upon an initial reading, include terms such as:

Ambassage, attend, beams, beck, blazon, bounty, charter, control, controlling, dear, due, duty, embassy, excel, flourish, glory, gold, golden, grace, gracious, heir, herald, high, honor, issue, jewel, largess, legacy, lord, master, might, mistress, ocean, ornament, pleasure, praise, presence, privilege, purple, right, rights, sea, seat, sit, slave, star, state, subjects, top, vassal, vassalage, we, will.

Holy Words

Princes are "gods on earth" or divinely ordained beings and, therefore, Southampton is depicted in the verses by many religious words. The Sonnets are sexual in the sense that their subject matter involves conception, birth and blood inheritance, but they convey a sense of spirituality to a greater degree than a sense of sexuality.

(The Dedication's reference to Southampton as the "onlie begetter" of the Sonnets, echoing the "onlie begotten Son" of the Bible, is an announcement of this spiritual or religious aspect. There are more than fifty distinct references to Biblical verses in the Sonnets.)

Some of the obvious "holy" words or phrases, as they appear in the Fair Youth series up to Sonnet 125, include:

Bears the Cross, Blessed, Blessing, Blest, Celestial, Consecrate, Creation, Eve's Apple, Feasts So Solemn, Forsake, Ghost, God, Goddess, Grace, Graced, Graces, Hallowed Thy Fair Name, Heaven, Heaven's Graces, Heavenly, Hell, Holy, Hymns at Heaven's Gate, I AM THAT I AM, Idol, Idolatry, Judgment, Lay Me On This Cross, Majesty, Miracle, Nativity, Oblation, Penance, Prayers Divine, Religious, Repent, Sacred, Sepulchers, Sin, Sinful, Sins, Soul, Spirit, Spirits, Three Themes in One, Un-bless, Zealous Pilgrimage

> That *every word* doth almost tell my name,
> Showing their birth, and where they did *proceed*
> Sonnet 76, lines 7-8

"Man shall not live by bread onlie, but by *every word*
that *proceedeth* out of the mouth of God."
Gospel of Matthew, 4.4

The 1609 Quarto

Thirteen copies of the 1609 quarto are known to exist; the fact
that most of these copies are in excellent condition, indicating very
little page turning by readers, supports the idea that they were never
distributed for sale at the time of their printing. Instead they would
have been in private mansions, waiting to be found.

All publications of authorized versions of Shakespeare plays shut
down after the authorized *Hamlet* (Q2) of 1604, the year of
Oxford's reported death, until the First Folio of 1623, which included eighteen newly printed plays among the thirty-six presented to
readers.

In 1608-1609, however, there was a sudden burst of unautho-
rized publications — *King Lear, Richard II* (with the deposition
scene for the first time) in 1608, and Pericles (which would not
appear in the First Folio) and *Troilus and Cressida* of 1609 — indicating, in my view, that Southampton was causing these works to be
issued along with the Sonnets.

Each of the plays published in 1608-1609 contains information
potentially pertinent to Oxford and the story of the Sonnets — a
matter for continued study. Included in *Troilus* of 1609 was a
strange and remarkable epistle from *A Never Writer to an Ever
Reader*, undoubtedly written earlier by Oxford, who accused "the
grand possessors" of refusing to publish the other Shakespeare plays.

If Oxford died later than supposed, in 1608, perhaps
Southampton felt the need to prompt Oxford's relatives to release
the texts of the plays that they held. In any case, King James went
into a panic on August 5, 1609, while on a hunting trip in

Southampton's territory, and asked for a special guard to be placed around him — supplied, ironically, by Southampton himself.

We inevitably come full circle, back to the narrative poems of "Shakespeare" that include *Venus and Adonis* of 1593, *The Rape of Lucrece* of 1594, *The Phoenix and the Turtle* of 1601 and *A Lover's Complaint*, which follows the Sonnets in Q of 1609.

The strong implication of the "monument" set forth here is that Oxford produced all these literary works to support Southampton and his political goals and to record his identity as a prince. I leave exploration of *A Lover's Complaint* for another time, except to suggest that it appears to offer another angle on the story of Oxford and Elizabeth – the early part, from the vantage point of the Queen herself. Most likely this work, too, is part of an overall plan.

Did Oxford really want to divulge to all his identity as Shakespeare? I think he would have wanted to continue operating behind the mask, at least during his lifetime and in the foreseeable future after his death. The great poetic and dramatic literature issued under the Shakespeare name was not written for his individual glory, but primarily for ongoing personal and political reasons culminating in the truth that he recorded for posterity in the Sonnets.

The irony is that, continuing to the end of his life under the Shakespeare name, Oxford was able to revise many of his works to include a myriad of aspects of his personal story for us – again, nonfiction dressed as fiction. Ultimately, I believe, he hoped that the Sonnets would lift the mask for posterity and, in that sense, that the "living record" of the monument would set him free.

Past, Present & Future

Alex McNeil, editor of *The Monument*, sums up what Oxford may have intended to tell Southampton:

• In my history plays, I wrote of the glories of England's former monarchs.

• My greatest hope, as your father, was that circumstances would permit you to claim your rightful place as Henry IX, succeeding Elizabeth. But I always knew this outcome was not certain.

• When circumstances turned out otherwise (as a result of the Cecils, Elizabeth's own state of mind, and finally the 1601 Rebellion), I concluded it was more important to try to save your life, even at the cost of renouncing your claim to the throne. If I can't make you King at the present time, I'll do what I can to make you King in the future, at least on paper.

• And so I left behind this monument, which contains the "living record" of you and your royal identity.

Chapter Eight

AN OVERVIEW

THE 100-SONNET CENTER
10 CHAPTERS OF 10 SONNETS

SOUTHAMPTON IN THE TOWER – *80 Sonnets*
1. CRIME   (27-36) Feb 8 – Feb 17, 1601
2. TRIAL   (37-46) Feb 18 – Feb 27, 1601
3. PLEA   (47-56) Feb 28 – March 9, 1601
4. REPRIEVE   (57-66) March 10 – 19, 1601

    [40 Days = 40 Sonnets]

5. PENANCE   (67-76) March 20 – 29, 1601
6. SACRIFICE   (77-86) March 30 – April 8, 1601
7. TEACHING   (87-96) April 1601 – Jan 1602
8. PROPHECY   (97-106) Feb 8, 1602 – April 9, 1603

    [40 + 40 = 80 Sonnets]

FINAL DAYS OF TUDOR DYNASTY – *20 Sonnets*
9. CONTRACT   (107-116) April 10 – 19, 1603
10. OBLATION   (117-126) April 20 – 28, 1603

    [80 sonnets + 20 sonnets = 100-sonnet center]

A SYNOPSIS — TIMELINE

1558: SUCCESSION:

Upon the death of Queen Mary I, Princess Elizabeth Tudor, 25, ascends the throne as Queen Elizabeth I of England. Her longtime supporter William Cecil becomes Principal Secretary.

1562: OXFORD THE FIRST ROYAL WARD

Twelve-year-old Edward de Vere becomes the first royal ward of the Queen in the care of William Cecil.

1571: OXFORD-CECIL MARRIAGE ALLIANCE

Elizabeth elevates Cecil from commoner status to Lord Burghley. Oxford, twenty-one, marries Burghley's fifteen-year-old daughter Anne Cecil, with the Queen attending the wedding and lending her support to the marriage.

1573: FIRST "SHAKESPEARE" SONNET

By now Oxford has composed the first English sonnet of the reign in the fourteen-line form that will be known later as Shakespearean. Entitled *Love Thy Choice*, it expresses his devotion to Queen Elizabeth and his commitment to serving her as a loyal subject.

1574: "THE LITTLE LOVE-GOD" (2 sonnets)

Oxford writes Sonnets 153 & 154 about his visit with Elizabeth and her Court to Bath in August, a few months after the birth of their unacknowledged royal son to be raised as Henry Wriothesley, Third Earl of Southampton. Oxford regards the infant son as a "god" on earth or king, who has been "disarmed" by his mother the Virgin Queen:

> The little Love-God lying fast asleep…
> Was sleeping by a Virgin hand disarmed
>   Sonnet 154

1575: BIRTH OF ELIZABETH VERE

Anne Cecil gives birth to her first child, Elizabeth Vere, while Oxford is traveling in France, Germany and Italy. Upon his return next year he will refuse to acknowledge paternity and separate from the marriage.

1581: HENRY WRIOTHESLEY A ROYAL WARD

Upon the death of the Second Earl of Southampton, seven-year-old Henry Wriothesley becomes the eighth and final royal ward of the Queen in the custody of Lord Burghley, while Oxford reunites with Anne Cecil.

1588: DEATH OF ANNE CECIL

Anne Cecil dies in June at age thirty-one, leaving behind three daughters: Elizabeth, Bridget and Susan.

1589: MARRIAGE PROPOSAL

Burghley initiates a proposal for his fourteen-year-old grand-daughter, Elizabeth Vere, to marry sixteen-year-old Henry Wriothesley. If the royal ward agrees to this alliance, Burghley will lend support for him to succeed Elizabeth. When Southampton becomes King Henry IX, his wife will become Queen and, through her, the Cecils will have achieved royal status.

THE FAIR YOUTH SERIES

1590-1600: "LORD OF MY LOVE" (26 sonnets)

SONNETS 1-17: 1590-1591

Oxford completes the first seventeen verses to Henry Wriothesley, coinciding with his son's seventeenth birthday, urging him to accept the Cecil proposal that he marry fifteen-year-old Elizabeth Vere, his daughter of record (but perhaps not his biological offspring) and Burghley's granddaughter. The opening lines, urging Southampton to propagate so Elizabeth's Tudor Rose lineage won't die with her, announce a dynastic diary:

> From fairest creatures we desire increase,
> That thereby beauty's *Rose* might never die
>> Sonnet 1

Henry Wriothesley rejects any alliance with the Cecils, however. In the coming years he will become closely allied with another royal ward, Robert Devereux, Second Earl of Essex (1566-1601), and they will challenge the influence over the Queen wielded by William and Robert Cecil along with their control over the succession.

These sonnets correspond with Henry Wriothesley's birthdays from age 1 in 1575 to age 17 in 1591. These "numbers" comprise "the living record" of him up to now; and the next nine will mark each birthday from Sonnet 18 (age 18 in 1592) up to Sonnet 26 (age 26 in 1600).

SONNET 18: PLEDGE OF SUPPORT: 1592

Remarried and withdrawn from public life, Oxford continues the dynastic diary with support of Henry Wriothesley in this golden time, represented as a "Summer's Day" of royal hope. The younger earl is bent on casting his lot with Essex against the Cecils in the endgame of political struggle to control the succession. Edward de Vere continues "the living record" of his son for posterity:

> So long as men can breathe or eyes can see,
> So long lives this, and this gives life to thee.
>> Sonnet 18

SONNET 19: "VENUS AND ADONIS": 1593

Oxford's newborn son by his second wife is christened "Henry" de Vere, the first appearance of that name in the 500-year earldom. A few weeks later he puts forth "William Shakespeare" in print for the first time, with his dedication of *Venus and Adonis* to Henry Wriothesley. The poem describes Southampton's birth as a "purple [royal] flower" to Elizabeth (Venus) and Oxford (Adonis). Henry Wriothesley is not only heir to the throne but also heir of the poem itself, as set out in the dedication:

"But if the first heir of my invention prove deformed, I shall be sorry it had so noble a godfather, and never after ear so barren a land, for fear it yield me still so bad a harvest..."

SONNET 20: "LUCRECE": 1594

Oxford puts forth "William Shakespeare" for the second time, with his public dedication of *Lucrece* (later entitled *The Rape of Lucrece*) to Henry Wriothesley, pledging his support:

"The love I dedicate to your Lordship is without end...What I have done is yours, what I have to do is yours; being part in all I have, devoted yours..."

Henry Wriothesley becomes Third Earl of Southampton, according to his "official" birthday in October, and gains the highest favor of the Queen, his mother.

SONNET 24: DEATH OF WILLIAM CECIL: 1598

Burghley dies at seventy-eight and his little hunchbacked son, Secretary of State Robert Cecil, assumes power over Elizabeth's government. Southampton marries maid-of-honor Elizabeth Vernon, a cousin of Essex, signifying his determination to win the power struggle against Cecil.

The poet "Shakespeare" is announced by Francis Meres as the author of popular plays performed at Court and on the public stage. Oxford, who has already linked Southampton to the pen name, thereby links his son to the stage works of "Shakespeare" as well, to increase his support of him.

SONNET 25: THE QUEEN'S DISFAVOR: 1599

Southampton and Essex return in defeat and disgrace from the Irish military campaign and find themselves in extreme disfavor with the Queen, a result that had been the aim of Secretary Cecil in the first place. Two verses in *The Passionate Pilgrim* this year will reappear in 1609 (in slightly different form) as Sonnets 138 and 144 of the Dark Lady series to Elizabeth.

Cecil solidifies his control over the Queen while Essex remains under house arrest and Southampton publicly associates himself with the "Shakespeare" works on the public stage.

SONNET 26: EVE OF REBELLION: 1600

Southampton and Essex, still in disfavor, begin plans to remove Cecil from his position of power over the throne and the royal succession.

Upon the disastrous Essex Rebellion of February 8, 1601, Oxford will conclude this first sequence of verses to Southampton with Sonnet 26 – having numbered them to represent the younger earl's twenty-six birthdays from 1575 to 1600 – by reaffirming his devotion to his royal son as a vassal pledging loyalty and duty to his king:

> Lord of my love, to whom in vassalage
> Thy merit hath my duty strongly knit,
> To thee I send this written ambassage,
> To witness duty, not to show my wit.
> Duty so great which wit so poor as mine
> May make seem bare in wanting words to show it.
>   Sonnet 26

THE "CENTURY" OF 100 SONNETS
AT THE CENTER

1601-1603: "MY LOVELY BOY" (100 sonnets)

"RICHARD II" AT THE GLOBE: FEB 7, 1601

With Oxford's consent, Southampton arranges for the Lord Chamberlain's Men to perform *Richard II* at the Globe, showing the deposition of an English monarch, to help rouse conspirators of the Rebellion. The play depicts Richard as a weak king who gives up his crown to Bolingbroke (Henry IV), as they hope the Queen will do.

After the Rebellion is crushed, Elizabeth herself will remark later: "I am Richard II, know ye not that?" But the author of the play, known as "Shakespeare," will never be called to account for his part in the uprising.

SONNET 27: THE REBELLION: FEB 8, 1601

The Rebellion against Robert Cecil fails; Essex and Southampton are imprisoned that evening in the Tower of London. Oxford begins a new series of sonnets to his now disgraced royal son, whose image appears to him as "a jewel hung in ghastly night."

SONNET 30: OXFORD SUMMONED: FEB 10, 1601

The Privy Council summons Oxford among the sixteen earls and nine barons to sit on the tribunal of peers at the "sessions" or treason trial of Essex and Southampton:

> When to the Sessions of sweet silent thought
> I summon up remembrance of things past...
> Sonnet 30

111

SONNET 33: "MY SUNNE": FEB 14, 1601

Filled with grief over Southampton's act of treason that has dashed any hope he might gain the throne, Oxford glances back at the birth of his royal son and the refusal of Elizabeth Regina to acknowledge him:

> Even so my Sunne one early morn did shine,
> With all triumphant splendor on my brow,
> But out alack, he was but one hour mine,
> The region cloud hath masked him from me now.
> Sonnet 33

SONNET 34: "RANSOM": FEB 15, 1601

As a member of the jury at the trial, Oxford will have no choice but to condemn his royal son to death; but he is pleading with Elizabeth and Robert Cecil, his brother-in-law, for the ability to pay a form of "ransom" to save Southampton, to whom he writes:

> Nor can thy shame give physic to my grief:
> Though thou repent, yet I have still the loss,
> Th'offender's sorrow lends but weak relief
> To him that bears the strong offence's loss.
> Ah but those tears are pearl which thy love sheeds,
> And they are rich, and ransom all ill deeds.
> Sonnet 34

SONNET 35: VOWING HELP: FEB 16, 1601

Oxford blames himself for having encouraged his son's "trespass" or treason by "compare," i.e., by writing the deposition scene of *Richard II* in addition to lending other public support with plays of "Shakespeare" for the public stage. Southampton has committed a "sensual fault" (a riotous, willful crime) against the state; Oxford must be his "adversary" at the trial, by voting to find him guilty of high treason, but will also be his "advocate" by sacrificing himself, to save his son's life and gain his ultimate release along with a royal pardon:

> All men make faults, and even I in this,
> Authorizing thy trespass with compare,
> Myself corrupting salving thy amiss,
> Excusing thy sins more than thy sins are:
> For to thy sensual fault I bring in sense,
> Thy adverse party is thy Advocate,
> And 'gainst myself a lawful plea commence
>> Sonnet 35

SONNET 38: THE TRIAL: FEB 19, 1601

Oxford appears at the head of the tribunal sitting in judgment of Essex and Southampton in Westminster Hall. The two earls are found guilty of high treason against the Crown and sentenced to death. In voting to condemn his own son, Oxford performed his political duty as a servant of the state; now he must perform his personal duty as a father and as the vassal of a royal prince.

SONNET 44: ESSEX EXECUTED: FEB 25, 1601

Robert Devereux, Earl of Essex is beheaded at the Tower of London, while Southampton remains in the prison. Robert Cecil is now without any rival in terms of his power behind the throne and his ability to engineer the succession of King James of Scotland. Trying to help Southampton, Oxford is forced to work with Cecil.

SONNET 55: "LIVING RECORD": MR 8, 1601

Anticipating Southampton's execution, Oxford is creating the most intensely sustained poetical sequence the world has known. It will become "the living record" of his son's royal claim for posterity:

Not marble nor the gilded monuments
Of Princes shall outlive this powerful rhyme...
Nor Mars his sword nor war's quick fire shall burn
The living record of your memory.
'Gainst death and all oblivious enmity
Shall you pace forth! Your praise shall still find room
Even in the eyes of all posterity
That wear this world out to the ending doom.
    Sonnet 55

Four other conspirators of the Rebellion are executed while Southampton waits.

SONNET 66: REPRIEVE: MARCH 19, 1601

Oxford records his profound emotional reaction to the Queen's sparing Southampton from execution. Behind the scenes, with maneuvering by both Oxford and Robert Cecil, she has commuted Southampton's death sentence to a term of life in prison as a base commoner. Knowing he will be forced to forfeit his son's royal claim, Oxford would prefer to die, but for the fact he would be leaving him alone in the Tower:

Tir'd with all these, from these would I be gone,
Save that to die, I leave my love alone.
    Sonnet 66

No public explanation for the reprieve is given, nor is any official record made, enabling Cecil to keep the death threat hanging over Southampton until Elizabeth dies and James VI of Scotland succeeds her as James I. Now Oxford must gain a further reduction of the judgment against his son in order to secure his eventual liberation and a royal pardon.

Now it has been exactly forty days since the first night of Southampton's imprisonment; and Oxford has kept pace by writing and compiling forty matching sonnets. In his mind, this anxious period has been akin to the forty days and forty nights of fasting in the wilderness by Jesus, who tells the Devil:

"It is written, Man shall not live by bread alone, but by *every word* that *proceedeth* out of the mouth of God"
Gospel of Matthew, 4.4.

This statement will be echoed by "*every word* doth almost tell my name,/ Showing their birth, and where they did *proceed*" in Sonnet 76; and having completed these forty verses from 27 to 66, Oxford is committed to building a "monument" for his son.

SONNETS 66-67 – CENTER OF PRISON YEARS
The first forty sonnets since the Rebellion, representing forty days, are now a yardstick by which Oxford will measure half the prison years; regardless of what length of time Southampton will spend in the Tower, there will be forty more sonnets to the point where he is either dead or free. Therefore Sonnets 66-67 now become the center of this sequence of eighty verses. Here is the center of an original monument positioned within the larger structure.

SONNET 67 – "WHY SHOULD HE LIVE?"
Southampton's life has been spared, but nonetheless Cecil will hold him hostage in the Tower until Elizabeth dies and King James of Scotland succeeds her as King James I of England. Oxford's immediate reaction is to wonder why his royal son must continue to live with "infection" or criminals in the Tower.

115

Ah, wherefore with infection should he live,
And with his presence grace impiety?
*   *   *   *   *

Why should he live…?
> Sonnet 67

SONNETS 76-77: THE "INVENTION"

Here, at what will become the exact midpoint of Sonnets 1-152 and of the 100 verses of Sonnets 27-126, Oxford pauses to describe his "invention" of writing and arranging the Sonnets, which revolves around "all one, ever the same" – Southampton, whose motto is *One for All, All for One*, and Elizabeth, whose motto is *Ever the Same*, along with *Ever,* a glance at himself as Edward de Vere or E. Ver. This "invention" employs "every word" from the "birth" of Southampton in 1574 to where his royal life has managed to "proceed" in the entries of this diary:

Why write I still all one, ever the same,
And keep invention in a noted weed,
That every word doth almost tell my name,
Showing their birth, and where they did proceed?
> Sonnet 76

Southampton and his "love," or royal blood, remain the constant "argument" of the Sonnets, so that Oxford must keep "dressing old words new" to continue writing about the same thing while avoiding the appearance of relentless repetition:

O know, sweet love, I always write of you,
And you and love are still my argument.
So all my best is dressing old words new,

Spending again what is already spent.
    Sonnet 76

He then dedicates "this book" to Southampton:

And of this book this learning mayst thou taste...
These offices, so oft as thou wilt look,
Shall profit thee, and much enrich thy book.
    Sonnet 77

SONNETS 78-86: THE "BETTER SPIRIT"

As Oxford bargains with Cecil behind the scenes, he begins the so-called "Rival Poet" series, recording his need to sacrifice and obliterate his identity as Southampton's father and, thereby as author of the Shakespeare works. His son will live in the Sonnets as King Henry IX:

Your name from hence immortal life shall have,
Though I (once gone) to all the world must die.
    Sonnet 81

He pledges again to build this "monument" to his royal son:

Your monument shall be my gentle verse,
Which eyes not yet created shall o'er-read
And tongues to be your being shall rehearse,
When all the breathers of this world are dead.
You still shall live (such virtue hath my Pen)
Where breath most breathes, even in the mouths
of men.
    Sonnet 81

SONNET 87: "MISPRISION": APRIL 1601

Oxford records the bittersweet bargain made for Southampton's life, involving the reduction of his crime from high treason to the "better judgment" of "misprision" of treason.

The lesser offense, allowing him to escape execution but requiring life imprisonment, paves the way for his potential release from the Tower and the restoration of his earldom. The "great gift" of his life will continue:

> So thy great gift, upon misprision growing,
> Comes home again, on better judgment making.
> Sonnet 87

The price to be paid is that Southampton must henceforth give up any claim to the throne:

> Thus have I had thee as a dream doth flatter:
> In sleep a King, but waking no such matter:
> Sonnet 87

SONNET 97: 1ST ANNIVERSARY: FEB 8, 1602

Oxford records the passing of the first "fleeting year" following the Rebellion of February 8, 1601, when his royal son began his imprisonment, echoing the Fleet Prison.

SONNET 104: 2ND ANNIVERSARY: FEB 8, 1603

Oxford records the passing of the second full year since the Rebellion, referring to the "three winters" since 1600, when the hopeful time for Southampton came to an end with Sonnet 26.

SONNET 105: QUEEN DIES: MARCH 24, 1603

Recording the Queen's death, Oxford refers to the fact that he,

Elizabeth and Southampton had "never kept seat" or sat on the throne as a royal family. Had he become King Henry IX, their son would have combined the blood of all three within his "one" royal person:

> Which three, till now, never kept seat in one.
>   Sonnet 105

King James VI of Scotland is proclaimed King James I of England, with Robert Cecil in full control of the royal succession while Southampton remains in the Tower.

ORDER FOR RELEASE: APRIL 5, 1603

According to the bargain made with Oxford and Cecil, and even before leaving Edinburgh to begin his triumphant journey south to London and the English throne, King James sends an order for the liberation of Southampton from the Tower.

SONNET 106: PRISON ENDING: APRIL 9, 1603

Oxford brings the "prison" verses to a close referring to his diary as "the Chronicle of wasted time." Referring to the recently deceased Queen as "Ladies dead," he predicts that Southampton will be Captain of the Isle of Wight and made a prestigious Knight of the Garter:

> When in the Chronicle of wasted time
> I see descriptions of the fairest wights
> And beauty making beautiful old rhyme
> In praise of Ladies dead and lovely Knights...
>   Sonnet 106

SONNET 107: LIBERATION: APRIL 10, 1603

Southampton emerges from the Tower. Oxford, referring to his son as having been "supposed as forfeit to a confined doom," celebrates his liberation. Elizabeth, who was Diana or Cynthia, goddess of the Moon, has "endured" her mortal decay by becoming immortal:

> The mortal Moon hath her eclipse endured...
>   Sonnet 107

The final twenty sonnets are arranged and numbered to correspond with the days up to and including the Queen's funeral, followed by his farewell to Southampton immediately afterward.

SONNET 125: FUNERAL: APRIL 28, 1603

Oxford records Elizabeth's funeral procession as her body is carried to its temporary tomb in Westminster Abbey, marking the "official" end of the Tudor Rose Dynasty begun by Henry VII in 1485.

Making his final "oblation" (sacrificial offering) to Southampton as prince or god on earth, Oxford also records his son is a "suborned informer" who – along with Time, which will become the official history – must testify against his claim to the throne.

SONNET 126: FAREWELL: APRIL 29, 1603

Oxford bids farewell to his royal son, promising that Nature – once Elizabeth, now "sovereign mistress over wrack" – will "render" him King in posterity:

Sonnet 126

O Thou my lovely Boy who in thy power
Dost hold time's fickle glass, his sickle hour:
Who hast by waning grown, and therein show'st

Thy lovers withering, as thy sweet self grow'st
  If Nature (sovereign mistress over wrack)
As thou goest onwards still will pluck thee back,
She keeps thee to this purpose, that her skill
May time disgrace, and wretched minute kill.
Yet fear her O thou minion of her pleasure,
She may detain, but not still keep her treasure.
Her Audit (though delayed) answer'd must be,
And her *Quietus* is to render thee.

    (   )
    (   )

THE DARK LADY SERIES

1601 – 1603 "TWO LOVES" (26 sonnets)
SONNET 127: THE REBELLION: FEB 8, 1601

Oxford begins this separate sequence, focusing on Queen Elizabeth, with twenty-six sonnets balancing the twenty-six-sonnet sequence that begins the Fair Youth Series. In terms of its time frame, the Dark Lady Series parallels Southampton's imprisonment until the Queen's death.

Sonnet 127 opens the series by focusing on Elizabeth's reaction to Southampton's disgrace for having committed high treason in the Rebellion. He was "fair" in the previous time of his life, but her Majesty's dark imperial frown has turned him to "black" as he faces execution.

To Oxford their son remains the Queen's "successive heir" to the throne, but, because of her viewpoint, she and her "beauty" (royal blood) that he carries are still "slandered" by the shame of bastardy:

In the old age black was not counted fair,
Or if it were it bore not beauty's name:
But now is black beauty's successive heir,
And Beauty slandered by a bastard shame.
    Sonnet 127

SONNET 145: REPRIEVE: MARCH 19, 1601

The imprisoned Henry Wriothesley is not only Oxford's son but an extension of his very being, so when the Queen spares the younger earl's life, it amounts to the sparing of Oxford's life as well:

Straight in her heart did mercy come...
And saved my life, saying, "Not you."
    Sonnet 145

SONNET 152: ELIZABETH DIES: MARCH 24, 1603

This is Oxford's final verse of the Dark Lady Series to Queen Elizabeth, who has died while leaving their royal son in the Tower, unable to claim his right by blood to the throne:

And all my honest faith in thee is lost.
For I have sworn deep oaths of thy deep kindness,
Oaths of thy love, thy truth, thy constancy,
And to enlighten thee gave eyes to blindness,
Or made them swear against the thing they see.
For I have sworn thee fair: more perjured eye,
To swear against the truth so foul a lie!
    Sonnet 152

Chapter Nine

THE ESSEX REBELLION

Attack on Southampton, Jan 9, 1601

Southampton is riding with his houseboy near Raleigh's residence when Cecil's henchman Lord Gray, accompanied by a band of followers, viciously attacks the earl. Southampton draws his sword and holds them at bay until help arrives, but not before the houseboy's hand has been lopped off. The Queen orders Lord Gray committed to the Fleet.

Turmoil at Essex House, Feb 2, 1601

Lord Gray is released today as frenzy grows at Essex's home near Temple Bar, with friends arriving in great numbers to support him and Southampton. At the same time their isolation from the Queen is leaving them increasingly defenseless. The release of Gray, undoubtedly at Cecil's urging, is further evidence that Essex and Southampton can no longer count on the protection of either Elizabeth or English law. Throngs of men come and go at Essex House. Rumors fly that the earls will soon be murdered, even in their beds. The pressure to take preemptive action is rapidly building to the boiling point.

Southampton Takes Charge, Feb 2, 1601

A committee headed by Southampton meets today at Drury House, the London residence of Sir Charles Danvers, to discuss plans for a palace coup. The committee will do the necessary staff work to plan the coming action, which will be aimed at getting rid of Robert Cecil and other enemies, such as Walter Raleigh, Captain of the Guard. These men will be taken as prisoners or, more likely, killed. Only then will the earls be able to gain Elizabeth's presence.

Essex has supplied a listing of 120 noblemen, knights and gentlemen who can be counted upon to help. Another document from Essex poses some questions about strategy. Should they seize control of both the Court and the Tower at once? How many men will be needed? If the attack is launched against the Court only, which places should be taken first? How many men should be assigned to control each area?

Second Meeting at Drury House, Feb 3, 1601

Southampton holds a second committee meeting. It's decided that the sole focus will be upon seizing the Court at Whitehall. Various members will infiltrate the Palace in advance. Individuals are being assigned to capture specific persons in specific areas. When committee member Sir Ferdinando Gorges expresses horror at the enterprise, saying the coup will be impossible, Southampton argues:

"Then we shall resolve upon nothing, and it is now three months or more since we first undertook this!"

The meeting breaks up in confusion, but Southampton is committed. He and Essex are convinced that hundreds of armed citizens will fly outdoors to join them. They also appear certain that once they come face to face with Elizabeth, she will recognize them as her loyal creatures risking everything for England's destiny.

Performance Arranged —Friday, Feb 6, 1601

Essex-Southampton followers approach the Lord Chamberlain's Men to arrange for a special performance of Shakespeare's *Richard II* tomorrow at the Globe. This powerful work is about the very real deposition and murder of King Richard in 1399, when Bolingbroke became King Henry IV of England. Its relevance to the current crisis must be obvious to the players.

Since all London has been talking for months about little else but the possibility of the Queen's own deposition, the actors must realize they are being used as a propaganda tool to further enflame the passions of conspirators and ordinary citizens alike.

Richard II at the Globe
Special Performance
Saturday, Feb 7, 1601

On this Saturday afternoon the Chamberlain's Men perform *Richard II* at the Globe, while members of the Essex faction cheer the scenes of an English monarch being deprived of his crown. Richard speaks:

"What must the King do now? Must he submit? The King shall do it. Must he be deposed?"

Oxford may have added the powerful deposition scene (4.1.154-318) to help Southampton's cause.

(Although the first quarto of *Richard II* was registered in 1597, the scene will be printed first in the fourth quarto in 1608.)

If such was the case, then Oxford may be referring to his own act of treason in Sonnet 35, lines 5-6:

"All men make faults, and even I, in this, authorizing thy trespass with compare…"

Apprised by spies of this event, Robert Cecil makes his own move. He sends John Herbert, his assistant secretary of state, to Essex House with a summons ordering Essex forthwith to attend an emergency meeting of the Privy Council, when he will receive instructions about how to conduct himself. By calculation the summons provokes the earl into even greater panic and confusion. He claims to be too ill to attend this meeting and refuses to leave his residence, which gives Cecil an opportunity to present Elizabeth

with more evidence of the danger she faces. If Essex is really so innocent of evil plotting, why won't he appear before the Council?

Tonight Essex and Southampton have dinner with Essex's sister,
Lady Rich, and with Sir Charles Danvers and his stepfather, Sir
Christopher Blount. Now that Cecil has taken the offensive, they
say, it might be best if Essex fled England. If he left with at least a
hundred men and made his way to Wales, he could take command
of a seaport and make a stand in his own defense. On the other
hand, the Sheriff of London has given his personal assurance of support by a thousand men of the militia; and the citizens can be
counted upon as well. So, they agree, there will be no flight by
Essex. The planned action must take place tomorrow.

Writes contemporary historian William Camden in his *Annales*
(1615, 1625):

"He [Essex] resolved therefore, for as much as delay was now no
less dangerous than rashness, to enter the next day, which was
Sunday, with 200 Gentlemen into the City a little before the end of
the Sermon at St. Paul's, there to inform the Aldermen and people
of the causes of his coming, and to crave their aide against his adversaries. And if the Citizens showed themselves hard to be drawn, to
depart presently to some other part of the kingdom; but if they
showed themselves easy, then to make himself a way unto the
Queen with their help. All that night some were sent out of Essex
House, who ran up and down to give his friends to understand that
the Lord Cobham and Raleigh [supporters of Robert Cecil] lay in
wait for his life."

The Rebellion
Sunday, Feb 8, 1601

The following excerpts are also based on, and drawn from,
Camden; with modernized English:

At Essex House resorted unto him (Essex) betimes in the morning upon Sunday the 8th of February, the Earls of Rutland and Southampton ... and about 300 Gentlemen of prime note. All these he courteously received and embraced.

To some he signified that a plot was laid for his life; that he was therefore determined to go unto the Queen and inform her of the dangers intended against him, for as much as his over-potent adversaries abused the Queen's name against him. To others, (he said) that the City of London stood for him; that he would therefore betake himself thither, and with the help of the Citizens revenge the injuries received from his adversaries. All this while his House kept shut, and no man let in unless he were known, nor any man suffered to go forth...

[Robert Cecil already has spies planted within Essex House; Camden implies that one is Ferdinando Gorges, who is permitted to go see Raleigh. In any case, warning is given to the government; and the following incident suggests a ploy by Cecil intended to provoke Essex into acting rashly before he is ready.]

At this very time the Queen gave commandment to the Lord Mayor of London to take care that the Citizens were ready every man in his house to execute such commands as should be enjoyned them. To the Earl (Essex) she sent the Lord Keeper, the Earl of Worcester, Sir William Knollys, Controller of her household and the Earl's uncle, and Popham Lord chief justice of England, to understand the cause of this Assembly.

These Councilors are hardly let in through the Wicket, their servants being shut, all save the Purse-bearer. In the Courtyard was a confused multitude of men, and in the midst of them Essex, with Rutland, Southampton, and many others, who presently flocked about them. The Lord Keeper, turning to Essex, gave him to understand that he and the rest were sent by the Queen to know the cause of so great an Assembly; and if any injury were done unto them by any man, he promised indifferent justice.

Essex answered him in a loud voice:

"There is a plot laid against my life; some are suborned to stab me in my bed; we are treacherously dealt withal; letters are counterfeited under my name and hand! We are met together to defend our selves and save our lives, seeing neither my patience nor misery can assuage the malice of my adversaries, unless they such also my blood!"

Popham spake unto him to the same effect that the Lord Keeper did, promising that if he would tell him plainly what had been attempted against him, he would report it truly to the Queen, and he should be justly and lawfully heard. Southampton made mention that the Lord Gray had drawn his Sword upon him. *"But he was imprisoned for it,"* Popham said.

Whilst the Lord Keeper pressed him (Essex) again to lay open his grievances unto them, if not openly, yet at least privately, the multitude interrupting him cried out:

"Let us go! They abuse your patience! They betray you and undo you! The time passeth!"

To whom the Lord Keeper, turning, commanded them upon their allegiance to lay down arms.

[All this confusion at Essex House leads to outright panic. Essex goes back inside, the Lord Keeper following in order to confer in private, while members of the crowd shout out:

[*"Let them be slain! Let that great Seal be thrown away! Let them be shut up in custody!"*

[And once the Crown's representatives are inside the house, Essex orders them taken as prisoners.

[*"Have patience a while,"* he tells the captives. *"I must presently be gone into the City to enter into some course with my Lord Mayor and the Sheriff. I will return by and by."*]

Essex through this unexpected coming of these Councilors forgot both horses and his design, and hastily went out of the house ... with a band of 200 men or thereabouts, all of them of age and courage fierce, but not provided of Arms like Soldiers, most of them having their cloaks wrapped about their arms and their swords…

Being entered into London, he cried out now and then:

"For the Queen! For the Queen! A plot is laid for my life!"

And so he went forward in haste directly through the chief street of the City to Sheriff Smith's house near Fen-church. The Citizens running together to gaze, he besought them to arm themselves, else they would be of no use to him.

Nevertheless in all the City, then well exercised to Arms, full of people, and most devoted to him, not so much as one man of the meanest sort took Arms for him. For the Citizens, though according to the disposition of the vulgar sort they were desirous of innovation, yet by reason of their wealth they were fearful withal, and in regard of their untainted fidelity to their Prince, unshaken…

[Most of the citizens, watching from windows and doorways, have no idea what is going on. For all they know, Essex is proclaiming his loyalty to the Queen.]

Having walked almost the whole length of the City to the Sheriff's house he came, much perplexed in mind, and in such a sweat that he was fain to shift his shirt. The Sheriff, in whom he had put assured confidence upon the uncertain credit of others, presently withdrew himself by a back door to the Lord Mayor…

[Agents of the government, under Robert Cecil's orders, now enter the city and begin to proclaim that Essex and his accomplices are traitors.]

When not a man took arms, and he saw that his own company withdrew themselves privily, and heard that the Lord Admiral was coming with a power of men, he began to cast away hope. He cast in mind therefore to return home, in hope to obtain favor with the Queen by the means of the Lord Keeper and the rest of the Council, whom he had shut up at home…[But it turns out that the captive Councilors have been let go!]

In the meantime Essex, being about to return, found the chain drawn athwart the street near the West gate of Paul's Church, and both pikes and shot placed against him by the Bishop of London under the conduct of Sir John Levison. Now the Earl first drew his sword.

He commanded Blount to set upon them; which he resolutely performed, running upon Waite ... Him he slew, and was himself sore hurt and taken prisoner. There fell Henry Tracy, a young Gentleman whom Essex loved dearly, and one or two citizens. From hence being repulsed, his hat shot through, and very many escaping from him, he turned aside (with a few which would not forsake him) ... and getting boats, returned home.

He was very much offended that the Council had been let forth. Certain papers he cast into the fire lest (as he said) they should tell tales; and prepared himself for defense. And now in his last hope, expecting aid from the Londoners, he fortified his house on all sides...

[Essex makes a final stand while government officials surround his house and high-ranking lords of the Crown prepare to lead a full assault. When calls come for Essex to give up, Southampton shouts back]:

"To whom should we yield? Our adversaries? That would be to run upon our own ruin! Or to the Queen? That would be to confess ourselves guilty! But yet if the Lord Admiral will give us hostages for our security, we will appear before the Queen! If not, we are every one of us fully resolved to lose our lives fighting!"

Before the hour was expired, Essex, holding all things for desperate and lost, resolved to break forth; and the Lord Sands, more aged than the rest, earnestly urged him so to do, redoubling that saying, "The stoutest counsels are the safest. It is more honorable for Noblemen to die fighting than by the hand of the executioner." But

Essex, wavering in mind, began presently to think of yielding, and signified certain conditions…

When presently all the Noblemen, falling upon their knees and delivering their swords to the Lord Admiral, yielded themselves at ten of the clock at night. Three died, no more but Owen Salisbury and one or two that were slain in the house by shot, and as many of the assailants.

Essex himself and Southampton were first led by the Lord Admiral to the Archbishop of Canterbury's house at Lambeth, and not straight to the Tower of London, because the night was foul and the bridge unpassable by water. But from thence shortly after, they were by the Queen's warrant carried by boat to the Tower; and in other boats Rutland, Sands, Cromwell, Mounteagle, Sir Charles Danvers and Sir Henry Bromley. The rest were cast in public prisons. Thus in twelve hours was this commotion suppressed, which some call a scare, others an error.…

They which (who) censured it more hardly termed it an obstinate impatience and desire of revenge, and such as censured it most heavily called it an inconsiderate rashness; and to this day there are but few which have thought it a capital crime.

Chapter Ten

THE PRISONER

Execution of Essex
February 25, 1601

On the night of February 24, 1601, Sir John Peyton, Lieutenant of the Tower of London, informed Essex he would die the following day. Because of his noble blood and high rank, he would not be hanged, drawn and quartered in public but, instead, beheaded in private. Between seven and eight o'clock the next morning, which was Ash Wednesday, Essex was led from his prison room to the Tower green.

Few of the peers who had been on the tribunal came to watch the execution, but more than a hundred others appeared nonetheless. Among the spectators was Walter Raleigh, one of Essex's enemies, who said he wanted to be able to answer any last-minute charges the earl might make against him. Others, however, felt he had come to "feed his eyes" on the sight of Essex's blood; and when they told Raleigh to move away, he withdrew to the Armory to watch from there.

Essex wore a black felt hat and black satin shirt covered by a black gown of wrought velvet. Approaching the low platform set up on a small square, he cried out:

"O, God, be merciful unto me, the most wretched creature on the earth!"

Then he addressed the high-ranking crowd:

"My Lords, and you my Christian brethren, who are to be witnesses of this my just punishment, I confess to the glory of God that I am a most wretched sinner, and that my sins are more in number than the hairs of my head!"

He confessed that *"this great, this bloody, this crying and this infectious sin, whereby so many for love of me have ventured their lives and souls and have been drawn to offend God, to offend their sovereign, and to offend the world, which is so great a grief unto me as may be!"* He prayed to be forgiven and asked God to bestow His blessing upon Elizabeth and her nobles and ministers, adding that he had never intended to bring about her death.

"It was not till the axe had absolutely fallen that the world could believe that Elizabeth would take the life of Essex. Raleigh incurred the deepest odium for his share in bringing his noble rival to the block. He had witnessed his execution from the armory in the Tower, and soon after was found in the presence of the Queen, who, as if nothing of painful import had occurred, was that morning amusing herself with playing on the virginals.

"When the news was officially announced that the tragedy was over, there was a dead silence in the Privy Chamber, but the Queen continued to play, and the Earl of Oxford, casting a significant glance at Raleigh, observed, as if in reference to the effect of Her Majesty's fingers on the instrument, which was a sort of open spinet, *'When Jacks start up, then heads go down.'* Everyone understood the bitter pun contained in this allusion. Raleigh received large sums from some of the gentlemen who were implicated in Essex's insurrection, as the price of negotiating their pardons."

Virginals: A "virginal" was a harpsichord-like instrument with jacks [pieces of wood fixed to the keyboard levers] that plucked at wires to produce sound. "How oft, when thou my music music play'st/ Upon that blessed wood whose motion sounds" – Sonnet 128

Her Majesty's fingers: "With thy sweet fingers when thou gently sway'st" – Sonnet 128

Jacks: "Do I envy those Jacks that nimble leap/ To kiss the tender inward of thy hand" – Sonnet 128

Cecil in Charge

"Elizabeth caused a declaration of the treason of Essex to be published, and a sermon very defamatory to his memory to be preached at St. Paul's Cross, by Dr. Barlowe, but the people took both in evil part. It was observed withal, that her appearance in public was no longer greeted with tokens of popular applause. Her subjects could not forgive her the death of their idol. Fickle as the populace have proverbially been considered, their affection for the favorite had been of a more enduring nature than that of the sovereign.

"The death of Essex left Sir Robert Cecil without a rival in the Court or cabinet, and he soon established himself as the all-powerful ruler of the realm. Essex had made full confession of his secret correspondence with the King of Scots, and also of the agent through whom it was carried on; and Cecil lost no time in following the same course." (Strickland, 675)

"The fall of Essex may be said to date the end of the reign of Elizabeth in regard to her activities and glories. After that she was Queen only in name. She listened to her councilors, signed her papers, and tried to retrench in expenditure; but her policy was dependent on the decisions of Sir Robert Cecil." (Stopes, 243)

"Thy adverse party is thy Advocate" is Oxford's pledge to Southampton in Sonnet 35, saying that while he must be his "adverse party" by voting to condemn him to death, he is also his "advocate" or lawyer helping him behind the scenes.

Southampton writes from the Tower to the Privy Council after his trial of Feb. 19, 1601, undoubtedly according to the advice of Oxford, who is acting as his "Advocate" or legal counsel -- possibly even written for him by Oxford himself:

"I beseech your Lordships be pleased to receive the petition of a poor condemned man, who doth, with a lowly and penitent heart, **confess** his **faults** and acknowledge his **offences** to her Majesty."

"Let me *confess*" – Sonnet 36

"All men make *faults*" – Sonnet 35

"To him that bears the strong *offence's* cross" – Sonnet 34

"Remember, I pray your Lordships, that the longest liver amongst men hath but a short time of continuance, and that there is none so just upon earth but hath a greater account to make to our creator for his sins than any **offender** can have in this world. Believe that God is better pleased with those that are the instruments of **mercy** than with such as are the persuaders of severe justice, and forget not that he hath promised **mercy** to the **merciful**."

"Excusing thy *sins* more than thy *sins* are"
     Sonnet 35

"The *offender's* sorrow lends but weak relief"
     Sonnet 34

"Straight in her heart did *mercy* come"
     Sonnet 145

"What my **fault** hath been your Lordships know to the uttermost, wherein, howsoever I have **offended** in the letter of the law, your Lordships I think cannot but find, by the proceedings at my trial, that my heart was free from any premeditate treason against my sovereign, though my reason was **corrupted** by affection to my friend [Essex] whom I thought honest, and I by that carried headlong to my ruin, without power to prevent it, who otherwise could never have been induced for any cause of mine own to have hazarded her Majesty's displeasure but in a trifle: yet I can not despair of her favor, neither will it enter into my thought that she who hath been ever so renowned for her virtues, and especially for clemency, will not extend it to me, that do with so humble and grieved a spirit prostrate myself at her royal feet and crave her pardon."

"For to thy sensual *fault* I bring in sense"
    Sonnet 35

"Loving *offenders,* thus I will excuse ye"
    Sonnet 42

"Myself *corrupting,* salving thy amiss"
    Sonnet 35

"O let her never suffer to be **spilled the blood** of him that desires to live but to do her service, nor lose the glory she shall gain in the world by **pardoning** one whose heart is without **spot**, though his cursed destiny hath made his acts to be condemned, and whose life, if it please her to grant it, shall be eternally ready to be sacrificed to accomplish her least **commandment**."

"When hours have *drained his blood*" –
    Sonnet 63

"To you it doth belong
  Yourself to *pardon* of self-doing crime"
    Sonnet 58

"How sweet and lovely dost thou make the shame
  Which, like a canker in the fragrant Rose,
  Doth *spot* the beauty of thy budding name?"
    Sonnet 95

"Commanded by the motion of thine eyes" –
 Sonnet 149, to Elizabeth

"My lords, there are divers amongst you to whom I owe particular obligation for your favors past, and to all I have ever performed
that respect which was fit, which makes me bold in this manner to
importune you, and let not my **faults** now make me seem more
unworthy than I have been, but rather let the misery of my distressed estate move you to be a mean to her Majesty, to turn away
her heavy indignation from me. O let not her anger continue
towards an humble and sorrowful man, for that alone hath more
power to dead my spirits than any iron hath to kill my flesh.

"My soul is heavy and troubled for my **offences**, and I shall soon
grow to detest myself if her Majesty refuse to have compassion of
me. The law hath hitherto had his proceedings, whereby her justice
and my **shame** is sufficiently published; now is the time that **mercy**
is to be showed. O pray her then, I beseech your lordships, in my
behalf to **stay her hand**, and stop the rigorous course of the law, and
remember, as I know she will never forget, that it is more honor to
a prince to **pardon** one penitent **offender** than with severity to pun-
ish many."

"With time's injurious *hand*" – Sonnet 63

"By a Virgin *hand* disarmed" – Sonnet 154

"To conclude, I do humbly entreat your Lordships to sound
mercy in her ears, that thereby her heart, which I know is apt to
receive any impression of good, may be moved to pity me, that I
may live to **lose** my life (as I have been ever willing and forward to
venture it) in her service, as your lordships herein shall effect a work
of charity, which is pleasing to God; preserve an honest man (how-

soever now his **faults** have made him seem otherwise) to his country; win honor to yourselves, by favoring the distressed; and save the **blood** of one who will live and die her Majesty's faithful and loyal subject.

"Thus, recommending my self and my suit to your Lordships' honorable considerations; beseeching God to move you to deal effectually for me, and to inspire her Majesty's royal heart with the spirit of **mercy** and compassion towards me, I end, remaining, Your Lordships' most humbly, of late Southampton, but now of all men most unhappy H. Wriothesley"

"If I *lose* thee…" – Sonnet 42

"Whereupon, [I am] willing to spend my time in her Majesty's service, to redeem the **fault** I had made in thinking that which might be **offensive** to her … my accursed fortune … I do therefore now prostrate myself at her Majesty's princely feet, with a true penitent soul for my **faults** past, with horror in my conscience for my **offences**, and detestation of mine own life if it be displeasing unto her. I do with all humility crave her **pardon**. The shedding of my blood can no way avail her … and do with so grieved a mind beg forgiveness … unfeignedly **repent** …"

"Though thou *repent*" – Sonnet 34

Southampton to Robert Cecil from the Tower:
"But now, seeing my chief hope is in your desire to effect my good … and I shall continue bound unto you, as I protest I do account myself already, more than any man living…"

Chapter Eleven

LIBERATION

Sonnet 107
My Love Looks Fresh

10 April 1603

Southampton, having been "supposed as forfeit to a confined doom" in the Tower, is released after spending twenty-six months in prison. Perhaps Southampton's release has also liberated Oxford's creative spirit; he will now return to composing a total of nineteen sonnets for the next nineteen days until the Queen's funeral on April 28, marking the formal end of the Tudor dynasty.

He refers to the death of Elizabeth ("the mortal Moon") and to the accession of James (now on his way to London) amid "Olives" of peace as opposed to civil war around the throne.

"My love looks fresh," he writes of Southampton, meaning that his royal son has retained his status as a prince even though he has forfeited the crown. Henry Wriothesley is still "the world's fresh ornament" as he had been in the very opening verse; and Oxford records this truth in his "monument" of the Sonnets so it may exist for the eyes of posterity.

This is the climax of Oxford's diary, with the three members of the family triangle represented: the author, Oxford; "my true love," Southampton; and "the mortal Moone," Queen Elizabeth.

Sonnet 107

1 Not mine own fears, nor the prophetic soul
2 Of the wide world dreaming on things to come

3 Can yet the lease of my true love control,

4 Supposed as forfeit to a confined doom,

5 The mortal Moone hath her eclipse endured

6 And the sad Augurs mock their own presage,

7 Incertainties now crown themselves assured

8 And peace proclaims Olives of endless age.

9 Now with the drops of this most balmy time

10 My love looks fresh, and death to me subscribes,

11 Since spite of him I'll live in this poor rhyme,

12 While he insults o'er dull and speechless tribes.

13 And thou in this shalt find thy monument

14 When tyrants' crests and tombs of brass are spent.

1 NOT MINE OWN FEARS NOR THE PROPHETIC SOUL

Neither my own apprehensions (about my royal son's fate in the Tower or about the succession of James) nor the anxious prophecies of others...

MINE OWN = characteristically used in relation to a son or daughter; "Tell me, mine own, where hast thou been preserved?" – *The Winter's Tale*, 5.3.123-124, Hermoine to her daughter; "a son of mine own" - Oxford letter to Burghley, March 17, 1575; so that here in this opening line, Oxford is referring to "fears for mine own son."

What can mine own praise to mine own self bring,
And what is't but mine own when I praise thee?
Sonnet 39

For term of life thou art assured mine
Sonnet 92

FEARS = dreads, doubts; things to be dreaded, objects of fear; "I was not sick of any fear from thence" – Sonnet 86, referring to those who claim victory over him and over the truth; "Then need I not to fear the worst of wrongs" – Sonnet 92, referring to his father-son bond with Southampton being stronger than his own mortal life

PROPHETIC SOUL = divining spirt; playing upon the "prophecies" of the previous verse (106) in which Oxford forecast Southampton's liberation: "So all their praises are but prophecies/ Of this our time, all you prefiguring,/ And for they looked but with divining eyes,/ They had not skill enough your worth to sing" – Sonnet 106

"O my prophetic soul! My uncle!" – *Hamlet,* 1.5.41

"Cry, Trojans, cry!
Lend me ten thousand eyes, and I will fill them with prophetic tears" – *Troilus and Cressida,* 2.2.102-103

"'Tis thought the King is dead ... The pale-faced moon looks bloody on the earth, and lean-look'd prophets whisper fearful change. Rich men look sad, and ruffians dance and leap – the one in fear to lose what they enjoy, the other to enjoy by rage and war. These signs foretell the death or fall of kings." – *Richard II,* 2.4.7

2 OF THE WIDE WORLD DREAMING ON THINGS TO COME

THE WIDE WORLD = England and beyond; the vast universe; "For nothing this wide Universe I call/ Save thou, my Rose, in it thou art my all" – Sonnet 109; "Thou that art now the world's fresh ornament" – Sonnet 1

DREAMING ON = predicting the future, both for England and for Southampton, as a result of the death of Elizabeth followed by the succession of James to the throne; "thinking about" or "speculating on" the possibility of civil war over the interchange of monarchs and dynasties; "the dreamer Merlin and his prophecies" – *1 Henry IV*, 3.1.144; having thoughts, visions, ideas, images in sleep

"O, Ratcliffe, I have dream'd a fearful dream! ... O Ratcliffe, I fear, I fear!" – *Richard III*, 5.3.213, 215

"O God, I could be bounded in a nutshell and count myself a King of infinite space, were it not that I have bad dreams" – *Hamlet*, 2.2.255-256, after Hamlet's characterization of Denmark/England as a prison

"Save that my soul's imaginary sight/ Presents thy shadow to my sightless view" – Sonnet 27; "But when I sleep, in dreams they [i.e., my eyes] look on thee" – Sonnet 42; "Thus have I had thee as a dream doth flatter:/ In sleep a King, but waking no such matter" – Sonnet 87; "Before, a joy proposed, behind, a dream" – Sonnet 129, to Queen Elizabeth, referring to the former hope that their son would wear the crown

THINGS TO COME = England's inevitable date with royal succession; the diary of the Sonnets has been a "dream" of that succession, i.e., Oxford's dream of Southampton becoming king; "Against this coming end you should prepare" – Sonnet 13

"Let this sad Interim like the Ocean [i.e., royal blood] be/ Which parts the shore, where two contracted new/ Come daily to the banks" – Sonnet 56

"That Time [mortal decay of Elizabeth] will come and take my love away" – Sonnet 64

"That you your self, being extant, well might show/ How far a modern quill doth come too short" – Sonnet 83

"My hour is almost come" – the Ghost of Hamlet's father, *Hamlet*, 1.5.4

3 CAN YET THE LEASE OF MY TRUE LOVE CONTROL

LEASE = the loan of royal blood to Southampton; the lease of Tudor Rose blood held by Queen Elizabeth, who has passed it on to Southampton by nature but not by will; "Nature's bequest gives nothing but doth lend" – Sonnet 4; "So should that beauty (royal blood from Elizabeth) which you hold in lease" – Sonnet 13; and in the Dark Lady series, near the end of the reign, to the Queen: "Why so large cost, having so short a lease,/ Dost thou upon thy fading mansion spend?" – Sonnet 146, referring to the rapidly expiring "lease" on her House of Tudor, which is now fading because of her refusal to release Southampton from the Tower and name him as her successor.

"A contract between parties, by which the one conveys lands or tenements to the other for life, for years, at will ... the period of time for which the contract is made ... with reference to the permanence of occupation guaranteed by a lease; esp. in the phrase "a (new) lease of life"; also, the term during which possession or occupation is guaranteed" – OED; 1586: "Of my graunt they had enjoy'd/ A lease of blisse with endlesse date" (Countess of Pembroke); 1628: "Remember of what age your daughter was, and that just so long was your lease of her."

"And our high-placed Macbeth shall live the lease of Nature, pay his breath to time, and mortal custom" – *Macbeth*, 4.1.98-99

MY TRUE LOVE = Southampton, my royal son; my true Prince; related to Oxford, *Nothing Truer than Truth*; "And your true rights be termed a Poet's rage" – Sonnet 17; "O let me true in love but truly write" – Sonnet 21

Bolinbroke: Go, some of you, convey him to the Tower.

Richard: O, good! Convey! Conveyers are you all,

That rise thus nimbly by a true king's fall.

Richard II, 4.1.316-318

CONTROL = have power over; a play on Southampton's own "controlling" as a prince, as in Sonnet 20: "A man in hew all *Hews* in his controlling"; "Never did captive with a freer heart cast off his chains of bondage, and embrace his golden uncontrolled enfranchisement" – *Richard II*, 1.3.88-90

"Yet looks he like a king: behold, his eye, as bright as is the eagle's, lightens forth controlling majesty" – *Richard II*, 3.3.68-70; "And Folly (Doctor-like) controlling skill" – Sonnet 66, referring to those in power who have controlled Southampton by leaving him in the Tower as a convicted traitor; (related to "controlment" or "controlling" of accounts)

Oxford uses the state "treasure" as a metaphor for his son's "account" of royal blood; in this context "control" extends the metaphor to its regulation by officialdom.

"In thy fayth I maye ... repose the controlement of my life"; 1604: "Otherwise the course of destinie were subject to our controlment" – OED: 1577

Here is a hand to hold a scepter up,
And with the same to act controlling laws
　　2 Henry VI, 5.1.102-103

4 SUPPOSED AS FORFEIT TO A CONFINED DOOM.

Presumed to be the victim of a life sentence in the Tower and also subject to execution at any time

SUPPOSED AS = imagined or thought (erroneously) to be; held as a belief or opinion to be; apprehended, guessed, suspected, intended to be; assumed to be true as; entertained as an idea to be; expected, obliged, taken for granted to be (or to have been); stated or alleged to be, as "formally in an indictment" - OED; "supposing by his writ" – OED, 1544

OED also lists the verb "suppose" as "to feign, pretend," and it may well be that Oxford intended the phrase "supposed as forfeit to a confined doom" to mean that Southampton was pretended to be doomed to confinement in the Tower for the rest of his life.

(This possibility occurs only when it becomes certain that James will succeed Elizabeth. Earlier, when Henry Wriothesley's life was spared, his fate remained uncertain and "supposed" would have correctly meant "generally believed.")

Having made the bargain for Henry Wriothesley to be liberated, few persons other than Oxford, Robert Cecil and King James would have known that the new sovereign would liberate Southampton; and so the earl was pretended to be confined for life.

"The maid ... was the daughter of his own bondswoman, who afterwards being stolen away, was carried to the house of Virginius, and supposed to be his child" – *Painter's Palace of Pleasure,* 1566, when Oxford was sixteen years old and very possibly involved in Painter's collection; ppl. adjective = believed to be; put on or feigned:

"Let the supposed Fairies pinch him sound..."
–*The Merry Wives of Windsor,* 4.4.61

FORFEIT = "subject to" and "legally owed to" – Kerrigan; "an act under whose heavy sense your brother's life falls into forfeit: he arrests him on it, and follows close the rigor of the statute to make him an example" – *Measure for Measure,* 1.4.64-68; OED 1594: "Forfeit and confiscate unto the crown"; and from 1495: "forfeitable ... to the Kyng"

"Claudio, whom here you have warrant to execute, is no greater forfeit to the law than Angelo, who hath sentenced him" – *Measure for Measure,* 4.2.156-159

Adjective: "That has been lost or has to be given up as the penalty of a crime or fault or breach of engagement."

(Upon the verdict at his trial, Southampton was condemned to have his life forfeited by execution; all his titles and lands were forfeited to – and confiscated by – the Crown. This was also the penalty to be paid by "misprision" of treason, which left him a perpetual prisoner without yet a royal pardon and, therefore, still subject to execution. King James will grant him the necessary royal pardon on May 16 this year.)

In the Dark Lady series Oxford pleads with Elizabeth on behalf of their son, offering his own life and honor as ransom for Southampton's liberation:

> So now I have confessed that he is thine,
> And I myself am mortgaged to thy will.
> Myself I'll forfeit, so that other mine
> Thou wilt restore to be my comfort still.
> Sonnet 134

"The King's further pleasure is ... to forfeit all your goods, lands, tenements, chattels and whatsoever" – *Henry VIII,* 3.2.337-344; liable to penal seizure, lost by breach of laws or conditions; given up for lost, forsaken

"And yet thy wealth being forfeit to the state, thou ... must be hanged at the state's charge" – *The Merchant of Venice,* 4.1.363-365

> Shall our coffers then
> Be emptied to redeem a traitor home?
> Shall we buy treason, and indent with fears
> When they have lost and forfeited themselves?
> *1 Henry IV,* 1.3.84-86
> There without ransom to lie forfeited
> *1 Henry IV,* 4.3.96

CONFINED = confined, imprisoned, in the Tower of London;

"So have we thought it good from our free person she should be confined, lest that the treachery of the two fled hence be left her to perform" – the King in *The Winter's Tale*, 2.1.193-196; possibly alluding to the "confinement" of Southampton's mother the Queen when she was about to give birth to him in May/June 1574.

> In whose confine immured is the store
> > Sonnet 84 (walled prison)
> A God in love, to whom I am confined
> > Sonnet 110

> Princes have less confines to their wills
> > OED: 1548
> "Denmark's a prison ... A goodly one, in which there are many confines, wards, and dungeons, Denmark being one o'th'worst"
> > *Hamlet*, 2.2.243-248
> Th'imprisoned absence of your liberty
> > Sonnet 58

OED: (confined) "Bounded, limited, restricted, restrained, shut up, enclosed, imprisoned"; (confine, verb) "to relegate to certain limits; to banish; to shut up, imprison, immure, put or keep in detention; to enclose or retain within limits ... keep in place"

> I am thy father's spirit,
> Doom'd for certain term to walk the night,
> And for the day confin'd to fast in fires,
> Till the foul crimes done in my days of nature
> Are burnt and purg'd away. But that I am forbid
> To tell the secrets of my prison-house
> > *Hamlet*, 1.5.9-14

So we have thought it good
From our free person she should be confined
    The Winter's Tale, 2.1.193-194

DOOM = judgment; prison sentence; Southampton's imprisonment and his possible execution; judgment of the trial and the Final
Judgment; the end or doom of the Tudor dynasty; "Norfolk, for
thee remains a heavier doom, which I with some unwillingness pro-
nounce. The sly slow hours shall not determinate the dateless limit
of thy dear exile; the hopeless word of 'never to return' breathe I
against thee, upon pain of life" – *Richard II*, 1.3.148-153, recalling
Southampton as "precious friends hid in death's dateless night" –
Sonnet 30; "Proud Bolinbroke, I come to change blows with thee
for our day of doom" – *Richard II*, 3.2.188-189; "Thy kingly doom
and sentence of his pride" – *Richard II*, 5.6.23

Thy end is Truth's and Beauty's doom and date
    Sonnet 14

In the Dark Lady series, Oxford writes of Elizabeth sparing their
royal son from execution:

Straight in her heart did mercy come,
Chiding that tongue that ever sweet
Was used in giving gentle doom
    Sonnet 145

Your praise shall still find room
Even in the eyes of all posterity
That wear this world out to the ending doom.
So, till the judgment that yourself arise,
You live in this, and dwell in lovers' eyes.
    Sonnet 55

This way the king will come; this is the way
To Julius Caesar's ill-erected Tower,
To whose flint bosom my condemned lord
Is doom'd a prisoner
    Richard II, 5.1.1-4

5 THE MORTAL MOON HATH HER ECLIPSE ENDURED,

MORTAL = "Such waste in brief mortality" – *Henry V*, 1.2.28;
"How many years a mortal man may live" – *3 Henry VI*, 2.5.29;
"Thou hadst but power over his mortal body; his soul thou canst
not have" – *Richard III*, 1.2.47-48; "O momentary grace of mortal
men" – *Richard III*, 3.4.96; also the sense of evil and/or deadly:
"Who 'scapes the lurking serpent's mortal sting?" – *3 Henry VI*,
2.2.15; "But I return his mortal foe" – *3 Henry VI*, 3.3.257

THE MORTAL MOONE = The mortal self of Queen
Elizabeth, known as Cynthia or Diana, Goddess of the Moon, i.e.,
her mortal body or physical self is dead, as opposed to her immor-
tal soul or spiritual self; "Making a couplement of proud compare/
With Sunne and Moone" – Sonnet 21, i.e., Southampton and
Elizabeth, son and mother; "Clouds and eclipses stain both
Moone and Sunne" – Sonnet 35, referring to the stain of disgrace
that the Rebellion has cast upon both Elizabeth and
Southampton, her royal son.

"Let us be Diana's foresters, gentlemen of the shade, minions of
the moon; and let men say we be men of good government, being
governed as the sea is, by our noble and chaste Mistress the Moon,
under whose countenance we steal" – 1 *Henry IV*, 1.2.25-29, an
obvious allusion to Queen Elizabeth for the contemporary audi-
ence; Elizabeth, also known as Venus, goddess of Love and Beauty:
"the mortal Venus, the heart-blood of beauty, love's invisible soul" –
Troilus and Cressida, 3.1.32-33

HER ECLIPSE = the Queen's "deprivation of light" (OED); her death, which has deprived England of her royal light, i.e., the same "light" possessed by her son, Southampton: "When thou thy self doth give invention light" – Sonnet 38

"Nativity, once in the main of light,/ Crawls to maturity, where-with being crowned/ Crooked eclipses 'gainst his glory fight" – Sonnet 60; so that this much-discussed line refers to Elizabeth as "the mortal Moon" who is already dead (as marked by Sonnet 105) and as the sovereign mistress who, simultaneously, has "endured" the "eclipse" of her light and glory on earth, as witnessed by mere mortals, by passing into the immortal, spiritual, eternal state of kings or queens; and in fact these are Oxford's sentiments as he expressed them to Cecil during this time:

"I cannot but find a great grief in myself to remember the Mistress which we have lost, under whom both you and myself from our greenest years have been in a manner brought up; and although it hath pleased God after an earthly kingdom to take her up into a more permanent and heavenly state (wherein I do not doubt she is crowned with glory) to give us a prince [James] wise, learned, and enriched with all virtues, yet the long time which we spent in her service, we cannot look for so much left of our days as to bestow upon another."

    - Oxford to Robert Cecil, April 25/27, 1603

Alack, our terrene Moon
Is now eclipsed, and it portends alone
The fall of Antony
Antony and Cleopatra, 3.13.153-155

Terrene = earthly, mortal
Moon = Queen Cleopatra, modeled upon Queen Elizabeth

Then here I take my leave of thee, fair son,
Born to eclipse thy life this afternoon.
Come, side by side together live and die...
   1 Henry VI, 4.5.52-54

ENDURED = sustained or submitted to; i.e., Elizabeth, being mortal, has died; but also being immortal, she is now in heaven; "to endure" also means to die, as in "Men must endure their going hence, even as their coming hither" – *King Lear*, 5.2.9-10, i.e., they must experience their deaths in the same way they had experienced their births; "Thou hast but power over his mortal body:/ His soul thou canst not have" – *Richard III*, 1.2.47-48

(Virtually all commentators agree that this line refers specifically and unambiguously to the Queen; and though debate continues over the dating, most also agree that the sonnet was written shortly after her death. See further discussion below.)

6 AND THE SAD AUGURS MOCK THEIR OWN PRESAGE,

And the gloomy prophets of civil war mock their own forecasts

AUGURS = those who practice the art of forecasting the future; "But thou shrieking harbinger,/ Foul procurer of the fiend,/ Augur of the fever's end,/ To this troop come thou not near" – *The Phoenix and Turtle*, 1601

"We defy augury. There is special providence in the fall of a sparrow" – *Hamlet*, 5.2.228-229, referring in Q2 of 1604 to the death of Elizabeth, who used the sparrow to identify herself

PRESAGE = foreboding, presentiment; "If heart's presage be not vain, we three here part that ne'er shall meet again" – *Richard II*, 2.2.141-142

O let my books be then the eloquence
And dumb presagers of my speaking breast
  Sonnet 23

So, hence! Be thou the trumpet of our wrath
And sullen presage of your own decay!
  King John, 1.1.27-28

7 INCERTAINTIES NOW CROWN THEMSELVES ASSURED,

INCERTAINTIES, etc. = the previous insecurities are now securities, i.e., "assured" of harmony and peace

CROWN THEMSELVES ASSURED = anticipating the crowning of James VI of Scotland as James I of England; "And in that chair where kings and queens are crown'd" – *2 Henry VI*, 1.2.38; "Anointed, crowned" – *Richard II*, 4.1.127; and Oxford in these verses will twist this monumental event into the crowning of his own royal son, Southampton: "Or whether doth my mind, being crowned with you,/ Drink up the monarch's plague, this flattery?" – Sonnet 114; and "But reckoning time, whose millioned accidents/ Creep in 'twixt vows, and change decrees of Kings/ … Crowning the present" – Sonnet 115

8 AND PEACE PROCLAIMS OLIVES OF ENDLESS AGE.

James offers a new era of peaceful prosperity;

OLIVES = King James used olives as a symbol of peace, both at home and abroad; "Olives" = "O. lives," or Oxford still lives; "Olive leaves or branches were an ancient emblem of 'peace' or security" – Evans; "And the dove came in to him in the evening; and, lo, in her mouth was an olive leaf pluckt off: so Noah knew that the waters were abated from the earth" – *Genesis*, 8.11;

PROCLAIMS = echoing the Proclamation of the Accession of James, which Oxford signed; "And once again proclaim us King of England" – *3 Henry VI*, 4.8.53; "I'll to the Tower with all the haste I can … And then I will proclaim young Henry king" – 1 Henry VI, 1.1.167-169; Evans observes this may be taken to suggest regal authority; right now the new king is taking his time on the triumphant approach to London and the throne (waiting until after the Queen's funeral procession to be held on April 28, 1603); but Oxford is well aware of the royal theme of the James progress: the king will enter "not with an Olive Branch in his hand, but with a whole Forest of Olives round about him" – Gervase Markham, *Honour in His Perfection*, 1624

9 NOW WITH THE DROPS OF THIS MOST BALMY TIME
NOW = at this very time of my royal son's release;

BALMY = this balmy spring; this healing quality (of medicinal ointment); the balm of kings, served to anoint the monarch; referring to the royal stature of Southampton while anticipating the coronation of James; "Not all the water in the rough rude sea can wash the balm off from an anointed king" – *Richard II*, 3.2.54-55

With mine own tears I wash away my balm,
With mine own hands I give away my crown,
With mine own tongue deny my sacred state,
With mine own breath release all duteous oaths;
All pomp and majesty I do forswear
—The King in *Richard II*, 4.1.206-211

"...the balm, the scepter and the ball, the sword, the mace the crown imperial" – *Henry V,* 4.1.256-257, i.e., aspects of kings; "The balm washed off wherewith thou wast anointed" – *3 Henry VI,* 3.1.17; "Balm was used in the coronation ceremony, and it was a familiar symbol of regal authority" – Kerrigan

10 MY LOVE LOOKS FRESH; AND DEATH TO ME SUBSCRIBES,

MY LOVE = my royal son; "If my dear love were but the child of state" – Sonnet 124; "In the devotion of a subject's love, tend'ring the precious safety of my prince, and free from other misbegotten hate, come I appellant to this princely presence" – *Richard II,* 1.1.31-34;

LOOKS FRESH = appears royal, as before he was imprisoned in the Tower; perhaps also suggesting that Oxford may actually have seen Henry Wriothesley upon his release, for the first time in many months (see previous sonnets, after the bargain is announced in Sonnet 87 – i.e., Sonnet 89 – alluding to a cessation of visits at the Tower). "Yet looks he like a king" – *Richard II,* 3.3.68; "Thou that art now the world's fresh ornament" – Sonnet 1; "since first I saw you fresh" – Sonnet 104;

AND DEATH TO ME SUBSCRIBES – and my son's expected death in prison now submits to me; Booth notes the legal echoes suggesting "to subscribe" as "to sign one's name"; Oxford has saved his royal son's life, behind the scenes, triumphing over death; in the process his son has given his word or "subscribed" to the bargain, by abandoning all claim to the throne; death also submits to Oxford by virtue of the fact that this monument of the Sonnets will defeat death: "'Gainst death and all-oblivious enmity/ Shall you pace forth!" – Sonnet 55

"From hence your memory death cannot take,/ Although in me each part will be forgotten./ Your name from hence immortal life shall have,/ Though I (once gone) to all the world must die" – Sonnet 81

11 SINCE SPITE OF HIM I'LL LIVE IN THIS POOR RHYME,

Because, despite my own death, I'll live in these eternal sonnets; but they are "poor" because Southampton has not been able to claim the throne and the Tudor dynasty is ending

I'LL = an echo of the "Isle" of Wight, where Southampton will become captain, and the "Isle" of Man, which James will return to the ownership and rule of Oxford's son-in-law William Stanley, Earl of Derby, husband of Elizabeth Vere; "I'll Live" suggesting that perhaps Oxford is planning to "live" on one of these islands in the near future.

12 WHILE HE INSULTS O'ER DULL AND SPEECHLESS TRIBES.

HE = death; INSULTS O'ER = triumphs over those who cannot (or will not) speak the truth; insult = exult, as a victorious enemy; "Ay me! I see the ruin of my House: the tiger now hath seized the gentle hind; insulting tyranny begins to jut upon the innocent and aweless throne" – Queen Elizabeth, wife of King Edward IV, in *Richard III*, 2.4.49-52;

SPEECHLESS = silent, dumb; dead; without means of speaking out, while Oxford, by contrast, is speaking here to future generations;

TRIBES = races, bodies of people having particular descents; the dead; echoing the "tribunal" upon which Oxford sat as highest-ranking earl at the trial; while proclaiming his own triumph over death, Oxford is also forecasting the victory of death over the current "speechless tribes" of men under the new reign, i.e., Secretary Robert Cecil, who will become Earl of Salisbury and run the Government until his death in 1612. These men have determined that death will bury Oxford in history, but he now defiantly retorts that "I'll live in this poor rhyme" – in the same way he has declared of the pen name "Shakespeare" that:

"He, nor that affable familiar ghost/ Which nightly gulls him with intelligence,/ As victors of my silence cannot boast!"

– Sonnet 86

13 AND THOU IN THIS SHALT FIND THY MONUMENT,

IN THIS = here in this Book of Sonnets; THY MONUMENT = eternal memorial; "Your monument shall be my gentle verse" – Sonnet 81; "Not marble nor the gilded monument/ Of Princes shall outlive this powerful rhyme" – Sonnet 55

"Again we see if our friends be dead, we cannot show or declare our affection more than by erecting them of tombs: whereby when they be dead indeed, yet make we them live, as it were, again through their monument. But with me behold it happenth far better, for in your lifetime I shall erect you such a monument that, as I say, in your lifetime you shall see how noble a shadow of your virtuous life shall hereafter remain when you are dead and gone" – Oxford's Prefatory Letter to *Cardanus' Comfort*, 1573

14 WHEN TYRANTS' CRESTS AND TOMBS OF BRASS ARE SPENT.

TYRANTS' = Elizabeth's = the tyranny of her "wasted time"; "But wherefore do not you a mightier way/ Make war upon this bloody tyrant time?" – Sonnet 16; "When in the Chronicle of wasted time" – Sonnet 106; the Queen's tyranny over her royal son; "But to prevent the tyrant's violence – for trust not him that hath once broken faith" – *3 Henry VI*, 4.4.29-30; "In act thy bed-vow broke and new faith torn/ In vowing new hate after new love bearing/ ... And all my honest faith in thee is lost" – Sonnet 152, Oxford to Elizabeth, at the end of the Dark Lady series, bitterly accusing her of breaking her promises to both him and Southampton

CRESTS = coats of arms on tombs of kings and queens; Elizabeth's crest carried her motto *Semper Eadem* or *Ever the Same*, as in "Why write I still all one, ever the same" – Sonnet 76

TOMBS OF BRASS = Elizabeth's temporary tomb in Westminster Abbey will rest "in the very shadow of the great tomb of Henry VII and his wife ... the most notable 'tomb of brass' in England" – Mattingly, PLMA 1933, p. 721; tombs of brass as opposed to the "tomb" of this "monument" of sonnets, which will outlive all such earthly tombs

Chapter Twelve

SONNET 107: COMMENTARY

(On the 1603 Dating)

Gerald Massey, 1866: "We may rest assured that [the Poet of the Sonnets] was one of the first to greet his 'dear boy,' over whose errors he had grieved ... He had loved him as a father loves a son; he had warned him, and prayed for him, and fought in soul against 'Fortune' on his behalf, and he now welcomed him from the gloom of a prison on his way to a palace and the smile of a monarch.

"Sonnet 107 will show us that, in spite of the dramatic method adopted by Shakespeare in writing of the Earl, he did find a call for secure congratulation when James had restored the Earl to his liberty. There can be no mistake, doubt, or misgiving here! This sonnet contains evidence beyond question – proof positive and unimpeachable – that the man addressed by Shakespeare in his personal sonnets has been condemned in the first instance to death, and afterwards to imprisonment for life, and escaped his doom through the death of the Queen.

"It tells us that the Poet had been filled with fears for the fate of his friend, and that his instinct, as well as the presentiment of the world in general, had foreshadowed the worst for the Earl, as it dreamed on things to come. He sadly feared the life of his friend – the Poet's lease of his true love – was forfeited, if not to immediate death, to a 'confined doom,' or a definite, a life-long imprisonment. The painful uncertainty is over now. The Queen is dead – the 'Mortal Moon hath her eclipse endured.' Cynthia was one of Elizabeth's most popular poetical names...

"Those who had prophesied the worst can now laugh at their own fears and mock their unfulfilled predictions. The new King calls the Earl from a prison to a seat of honor ... Our Poet evidently hopes that the Earl's life will share in this new dawn of gladness and promised peace of the nation. He can exult over death this time. It is his turn to triumph now. And his friend shall find a monument in his verse which shall exist when the crests of tyrants have crumbled and their brass-mounted tombs have passed from sight ... The sonnet carries double. It blends the Poet's private feeling for his friend with the public fear for the death of the Queen. The 'Augurs' had contemplated that event with mournful forebodings, and prophesied changes and disasters ... But it has passed over happily for the nation as joyfully for the Poet."

—*Shakespeare's Sonnets Never Before Interpreted,*
    pp 79 and 311-313

Sidney Lee, 1898: "Sonnet 107 ... makes references that cannot be mistaken to three events that took place in 1603 – to Queen Elizabeth's death, to the accession of James I, and to the release of the Earl of Southampton, who had been in prison since he was convicted in 1601 of complicity in the rebellion of the Earl of Essex ... Elizabeth's crown had been passed, without civil war, to the Scottish King, and thus the revolution that had been foretold as the inevitable consequence of Elizabeth's demise was happily averted ...

"There was hardly a verse-writer who mourned her loss that did not typify it, moreover, as the eclipse of a heavenly body ... At the same time James was constantly said to have entered on his inheritance 'not with an olive branch in his hand, but with a whole forest of olives round about him, for he brought not peace to this kingdom alone' but to all Europe ...

"'The drops of this most balmy time,' in this same sonnet, 107, is an echo of another current strain of fancy. James came to England in a springtide of rarely rivaled clemency, which was reckoned of the happiest augury ... One source of grief alone was acknowledged: Southampton was still a prisoner in the Tower, 'supposed as forfeit to a confined doom.' All men, wrote Manningham, the diarist, on the day following the Queen's death, wished him liberty. The wish was fulfilled quickly. On April 10, 1603, his prison gates were opened by 'a warrant from the king' ... It is improbable that Shakespeare remained silent. 'My love looks fresh,' he wrote, in the concluding lines of Sonnet 107, and he repeated the conventional promise that he had so often made before, that his friend should live in his 'poor rhyme,' 'when tyrants' crests and tombs of brass are spent.'"

– *A Life of William Shakespeare,* pp. 147-150

Garrett Mattingly, 1933: "Critics have generally agreed that, of all of Shakespeare's sonnets, 107 offers the most hope for dating by internal evidence. Since Massey first argued the point in 1866 a number of distinguished scholars ... have supported the view that this sonnet refers to the death of Queen Elizabeth and the accession of James I... That Elizabeth is meant by 'the mortal moon' there can be no reasonable doubt. All her life she had been Cynthia ... In a general way it has always been clear that the events of the spring of 1603 do satisfy the conditions ... The further such an inquiry is pushed, the more striking becomes the evidence that the second quatrain of the sonnet expresses exactly the state of mind of most of Shakespeare's contemporaries ... and the stronger becomes the conviction that, of all the public events of Shakespeare's lifetime, these are the most likely to find an echo in the sonnets.

"To the average Elizabethan Englishman, at least, the greatest crisis of Elizabeth's reign was that which marked its close. To him, the certainty and security of the succession to the throne came first ... No one had forgotten the Wars of the Roses, and the corollary of a disputed succession was civil war ... A dread of civil war explains more than half of England's loyalty to the Tudors.

"And, as the century drew to a close, men perceived that the last of the Tudors would die without issue, and nothing settled ... But James was a foreigner, and lawyers were found to argue that if birth in a foreign kingdom and status as the subject of a foreign crown could bar claimants from the inheritance of land in England (as under the law it did), then surely such birth barred succession to the throne...

"(The) real danger of a disputed succession ... was widely appreciated and formed the basis of the gloomiest prophecies. Shakespeare could not have been ignorant of it or indifferent to it. His plays ... do show a keen interest in dynastic questions ... Indeed, few people either in England or in Scotland expected James to accede peaceably ... It is rather to the peaceable union with the enemy, Scotland, and to the apparently permanent relief from danger of civil war that the phrase 'olives of endless age' is to be applied; but James's accession extinguished the last sparks of trouble in Ireland, and peace with Spain, too, was seen in the offing. Hostilities with Spain were suspended on James I's accession, for he held that, as in his capacity of King of Scotland he was not at war with that power, he could not be at war with her as King of England...

"The more one closely examines the events of the spring of 1603, as they were seen by Shakespeare's contemporaries, the more consistent do they appear with the language of Sonnet 107, even in its slightest details, and the more likely does it seem that these events would have impressed the poet deeply enough to find a record in the sonnets. Nor do the allusions in the sonnet seem appropriate to any other sequence of public events during Shakespeare's lifetime."

- PLMA, XLVIII, 1933, pp. 705-721

Alfred Harbage, 1950: "All that we know certainly of Sonnets 107, 123 and 124 is that they were published in 1609 ...Their style – by which is meant here their music and the condensation and integration of their language – suggests to me that they were written late rather than early in Shakespeare's career ... The early months of 1603 were among the blackest in English history: there was fear of Tyrone in Ireland, and of masterless men and malcontents in England: the Queen was dying and her successor unnamed; forty thousand Catholics were said to be ready to rise in arms if the successor should be James ... Then, as if by miracle, the crisis passed, and James ascended the English throne in an almost hysterical outburst of national joy ... the astrological and historical background of 1603 was appropriate for the allusions in Sonnet 107 ... If we can speak of such a thing as a season of imagery, this was the season of heavenly bodies, setting, rising, eclipsed, etc., and the season of olives of endless age.

"The moon had always been Elizabeth's symbol. She had been Cynthia herself, or, as in Shakespeare, Cynthia's 'imperial vot'ress.' In the elegiac chorus of 1603, she is Luna, Delia, Cynthia, Phoebe, Belphoebe (all the moon), or else the setting sun ... In the presence of Death, Elizabeth qualified poetically as a tyrant ... (Shakespeare's) voice is missing among the poetic eulogists of Elizabeth and James in the 'Wonderful Year' (1603). The tone (of Sonnets 107, 123 and 124) ... suggests to me a man quite willing to 'sit out' the public excitements over a change in administration."
– *Shakespeare Quarterly*, Vol.1, no. 2, April 1950, 57-63

G. P. V. Akrigg, 1968: "H. C. Beeching ... declared 'the only sonnet that can be dated with absolute certainty from internal evidence (107) belongs to 1603.' Dover Wilson ... has continued to recognize that Sonnet 107 dates from 1603 ... Re-reading Sonnet 107 in another connection ... I had a sudden complete conviction that the sonnet belonged to 1603, almost as if it had the date visibly branded upon it ... This is what Shakespeare had to say to Southampton upon his release from imprisonment:

"'I myself in my fears had thought, like everybody else, that the future held nothing for you beyond continued confinement in the Tower.

"'But now Queen Elizabeth, so often likened to Cynthia, the virgin goddess of the moon, has finally been eclipsed by death. Since she had no acknowledged heir, pessimists had feared that her passing would bring a disastrous civil war, but now even they mock their earlier dismal prophecy.

"'With the peaceful accession of King James, feelings of uncertainty give way to feelings of security. Our new King, dedicated to peace, brings us an unending era of peace and prosperity. The refreshing showers of this pleasant spring give new vigor to my love for you. Poor though my verse may be, it forces death to submit to me. I shall attain a literary immortality denied to the inarticulate masses.

"'And this poetry of mine will provide you with a monument which will keep you remembered when elaborate tombs, like that to be raised for our late tyrannical Queen, have disappeared.'"
– *Shakespeare and the Earl of Southampton*, pp 254-255

Robert Giroux, 1982: "This sonnet (107) could not have been written before 24 March 1603, the date of Queen Elizabeth's death, for a good reason: the word 'tyrant' was risky to put on paper at any time during her reign, and mortally dangerous if coupled with a reference to her. It is generally agreed that 'mortal Moon' refers to Elizabeth ... ('Men must endure their going hence, even as their coming hither. Ripeness is all" – *King Lear*, 5.2.9-11) Men must endure their deaths, even as their births; ripeness is all there is. 'Endure' can of course mean survive, but the O. E. D. also defines it as 'to suffer without resistance, to submit to, to undergo,' and that is how Shakespeare uses the word in both places. By 'the mortal Moon hath her eclipse endured,' Shakespeare means that, as a mortal, the Queen has undergone death. '*Her* eclipse' instead of '*an* eclipse ... further emphasizes a permanent rather than a temporary state...

"There is nothing anywhere else in the sonnets like the mastery and freedom of the first quatrain (of 107) ... This single sentence, one marvelous breath, could only have been written by a poet in the fullness of his powers ... Other historical allusions in this sonnet place the poem solidly in 1603 ... At Southampton's trial, it had been remarked how youthful he still looked. On his release from the Tower in April 1603, he was in his twenty-ninth year ('my love looks fresh')"

– *The Story of Q,* pp. 191-198

John Kerrigan, 1986: "[In Sonnet 107] the present events are realized so vividly that they can be read as topical allusions ... Any dating of the poet's change of heart can be linked to the public events described in lines 5-9, as either written at the time or, less likely, retrospectively set in that context. And this means that, if the allusions are unlocked, they probably date the poem, and certainly set a terminus a quo for its composition...

"A considerable outburst of anxious astrology and prediction ... preceded the Queen's death. As her health worsened and the political picture remained obscure, foreboding grew. Much was at stake. Elizabeth had announced no successor, and both Catholics and Puritans feared the accession of a ruler less sympathetic to their religious liberty than the moderate Protestant Queen had been. More than a dozen claimants maintained their right to the throne ... and the people anticipated either invasion from abroad or civil strife of the kind which laid the country waste during the Wars of the Roses, before Tudor settlement...

"In the light of the secondary sense of 'My love looks fresh' it is remarkable that one of the first acts of the newly-crowned King [well before the coronation] was to release the Earl of Southampton, often thought the addressee of Sonnets 1-126, from the prison in which he had languished ever since his participation in the ill-fated Essex Rebellion of 1601. If Wriothesley was indeed, to some emotional extent, the *you* and *thou* and *love* of 1-126, both he and the poet's affection for him would have been refreshed and renewed by the events of 1603... On the basis of allusions, in short, 1603 seems the obvious date – with all which that implies for the dating of the sequence ..."

– *The Sonnets and A Lover's Complaint*, Penguin, pp. 313-320

G. Blakemore Evans, 1996: "The majority of recent critics strongly favours 1603 as the most likely date. Indeed, the case for 1603 (or a little later) is so brilliantly presented by Kerrigan that one is dangerously tempted to cry 'Q. E. D.'"

– *The Sonnets*, pp. 216-217

Chapter Thirteen

AWAITING EXECUTION

Dark Lady Series
Sonnet 133
Of Him, My Self, And Thee,
I Am Foresaken
March 1601

The Dark Lady Series (127-152) covers the same time period as the eighty prison sonnets (27-106) of the much longer Fair Youth Series (1-126). Therefore Sonnet 133 takes us back to when Southampton has been in the Tower for more than a month and may be executed at any moment.

Oxford fills this sonnet of the Dark Lady series (addressed to Queen Elizabeth) with images of the Tower prison where his "next self" waits: "Prison ... ward (guard) ... bail ... guard ... Jail ... pent." He suffers increasingly as the time for the Queen's decision draws near, wondering whether she will give the order for Southampton's execution as she had for Essex.

His "groan" is that of the funeral moan for his royal son; and this verse alludes to the suffering of Christ; its number, 133, echoes that of the "resurrection" verse, Sonnet 33. It is also the age of Christ upon His death on the Cross. It recalls Sonnet 34: "Th'offender's sorrow lends but weak relief to him that bears the strong offence's loss." It also recalls his statement about Elizabeth and Southampton in Sonnet 42: "And both for my sake lay on me this cross."

> So now I have confessed that he is thine
> And I myself am mortgaged to thy will,

My self I'll forfeit, so that other mine
Thou wilt restore, to be my comfort still.
Sonnet 134

"This verse [134] clearly refers to the confinement of Southampton in the Tower and the former verse [133] expresses the Poet's desire to be permitted to go his bail, by substituting his own person for that of his friend, in jail … The Poet here proffers to forfeit himself as security for his friend…" - *Commentaries on the Law in Shakespeare*, 1911, Edward Joseph White, pp. 511-12

Sonnet 133

1 Beshrew that heart that makes my heart to groan
2 For that deep wound it gives my friend and me.
3 Is't not enough to torture me alone,
4 But slave to slavery my sweet'st friend must be?
5 Me from my self thy cruel eye hath taken,
6 And my next self thou harder hast engrossed.
7 Of him, my self, and thee, I am forsaken,
8 A torment thrice three-fold thus to be crossed:
9 Prison my heart in thy steel bosom's ward,
10 But then my friend's heart let my poor heart bail,
11 Who ere keeps me, let my heart be his guard,
12 Thou canst not then use rigor in my Jail.
13 And yet thou wilt, for I being pent in thee,
14 Perforce am thine, and all that is in me.

1 BESHREW THAT HEART THAT MAKES MY HEART TO GROAN

BESHREW = "Fie upon" - Booth; curse the cruelty of that cruel heart (Elizabeth's royal heart) that makes my own heart groan in anticipation of our son's death; referring back to "Knowing thy heart torment me with disdain" – Sonnet 132, and preparing for "torment" of line 8 below

GROAN = same as "moan" as in "a great groan (was) made for him" – report in Machyn's Diary of the funeral for Edward de Vere's father, the 16th Earl of Oxford, on August 31, 1562; ("groaning for burial" – *Julius Caesar*, 3.1.275)

MY HEART = "my heart" is my dear son; to Southampton: "Take heed, dear heart, of this large privilege" – Sonnet 95

2 FOR THAT DEEP WOUND IT GIVES MY FRIEND AND ME.

DEEP WOUND = suggesting the wounds of Christ upon the Cross; MY FRIEND AND ME = my son and me; "I am good friends with my father" – *1 Henry IV*, 3.3.182; MY FRIEND = my son, Southampton; "For precious friends hid in death's dateless night" – Sonnet 30; "But being both from me both to each friend" – Sonnet 144

3 IS'T NOT ENOUGH TO TORTURE ME ALONE,

ALONE = the "all" and "one" of Southampton, *One for All, All for One*; ME ALONE = Oxford alone, but also both Oxford and Southampton, with whom he equates himself; IS'T NOT ENOUGH TO TORTURE ME ALONE = a rhetorical utterance Oxford may have made in person to Elizabeth; alluding to Christ-like suffering; "And each, though enemies to each other's reign,/ Do in consent shake hands to torture me" – Sonnet 28; echoing his son's imprisonment and the torture (often on the "rack") that was routinely used in Elizabethan prisons

4 BUT SLAVE TO SLAVERY MY SWEET'ST FRIEND MUST BE?

FRIEND = repeated from line 2; Oxford also may have spoken this line directly to Elizabeth: "But must my most royal son also be a slave to your slavery?" SLAVE = a servant to the monarch and/or a prisoner; ("a base and contemptible person" – Booth); i.e., Southampton imprisoned and in disgrace; MY SWEET'ST FRIEND = my most royal son; "sweet boy" – Sonnet 108

5 ME FROM MY SELF THY CRUEL EYE HATH TAKEN,

Your cruel royal attitude (or viewpoint or decree) has taken me from my own son, who is my own self; THY CRUEL EYE = Elizabeth's all-powerful, imperial eye, casting its shadow over her son; "But found no cure; the bath for my help lies/ Where Cupid got new fire, my mistress' eye" – Sonnet 153; TAKEN = taken from Oxford, the father, and imprisoned

6 AND MY NEXT SELF THOU HARDER HAST ENGROSSED.

MY NEXT SELF = an extension of the thought, with Southampton now viewed as Oxford's second self; as he writes to his son: "Make thee another self for love of me" – Sonnet 10; "'Tis thee, my self, that for my self I praise" – Sonnet 62; "the second burden of a former child" – Sonnet 59

THOU HARDER HATH ENGROSSED = you have more severely taken possession of, i.e., of his son; "That she hath thee is of my wailing chief" – Sonnet 42, also written during this time;

ENGROSSED = having him in her prison, i.e., the Tower

7 OF HIM, MY SELF, AND THEE, I AM FORSAKEN,

The royal family of Southampton, Oxford and Elizabeth, echoing the Holy Trinity, as well as Christ on the Cross; i.e., Oxford is suffering, but will sacrifice his own life or identity; echoing "I am that I am," the words of God to Moses, used in Sonnet 121

8 A TORMENT THRICE THREEFOLD THUS TO BE CROSSED

A torment suffered by each of the three of us, and also three times again by all three together

THREEFOLD = "Three themes in one, which wondrous scope affords/ ... Which three, till now, never kept seat in one" – Sonnet 105; "And thou treble-dated crow ... Beauty, Truth, and Rarity" – *The Phoenix and Turtle*, 1601

CROSSED = all three suffering on the Cross; "And both for my sake lay on me this cross" – Sonnet 42

9 PRISON MY HEART IN THY STEEL BOSOM'S WARD,

PRISON = alluding to Southampton's imprisonment in the Tower; MY HEART IN THY STEEL BOSOM'S WARD = you have our son in prison, but I ask you to imprison my own heart instead, within the steel gates of your bosom; STEEL = cold heart, but the steel bars of a prison; WARD = "prison cell; guard, custody" – Booth

10 BUT THEN MY FRIEND'S HEART LET MY POOR HEART BAIL:

BUT THEN, etc. = after imprisoning me, let me pay for my son's crime by bailing him out of prison; BAIL = bail out or redeem; "Justices of the Peace might ... have letten to baile such persons as were indited of Felonie" – OED, from 1581 (cited by Booth); also used as "to confine" or to imprison or to guard; and so, also, let him be confined in my heart instead

11 WHO ERE KEEPS ME, LET MY HEART BE HIS GUARD,

WHO ERE KEEPS ME = whoever holds me in prison; the queen or his son, who is "a God in love, to whom I am confined" – Sonnet 110; GUARD = echoing his royal son's imprisonment; LET MY HEART BE HIS GUARD = let me be his jailer

12 THOU CANST NOT THEN USE RIGOR IN MY JAIL.

JAIL = alluding to Southampton's confinement in the Tower; THOU CANST NOT THEN USE RIGOR IN MY JAIL = ("Jaile" is capitalized in Q); so long as he is in my jail, you cannot execute him as the law requires; (as opposed to him being in your jail, the Tower of London)

RIGOR = (spelled this way in Q); "strict enforcement of a law" – Booth; harsh, recalling "extreme" of Sonnet 129; "I tell you 'tis rigour and not law" – *The Winter's Tale*, 3.2.112; "Let him have all the rigour of the law" – *2 Henry VI*, 1.3.190

13 AND YET THOU WILT, FOR I BEING PENT IN THEE,

PENT = echoing Southampton's imprisonment; "A liquid prisoner pent in walls of glass" – Sonnet 5, showing that Oxford had already used "pent" in relation to prison; PENT IN THEE = imprisoned within you and by you, Elizabeth, my sovereign; by keeping our son in jail, you have me in prison, too.

14 PERFORCE AM THINE, AND ALL THAT IS IN ME.

Of necessity I am your prisoner; PERFORCE = to force, constrain, oblige; "The present pains perforce, that love aye seeks" –

Oxford poem, *The Paradise of Dainty Devices*, 1576; "Patience perforce is such a pinching pain" – Earl of Oxenforde, Tanner MS 306,
f. 115; Chiljan, 186

ALL = Southampton, *One for All, All for One*; he, too, is your
prisoner; ALL THAT IS IN ME = "In imprisoning me, you are
imprisoning all that is in me, and he is in my heart; therefore, whatever harshness you show to me affects him also, and I shall feel for
him any rigour which I should not feel for myself" – Tucker;
Southampton, our son, is all that is within me; you have both of us:
"That she hath thee is of my wailing chief" – Sonnet 42, Oxford as
chief mourner addressing his son.

Chapter Fourteen

OXFORD IN THE SONNETS

Biographical Footprints

Edward de Vere, Earl of Oxford (1550-1604) was in the best position of anyone in England to write the Shakespeare sonnets. Here is a list of some links to his life:

THE POET SURREY

Oxford's uncle was the Henry Howard, Earl of Surrey (1517-1547), who (with Sir Thomas Wyatt) wrote the first English sonnets in the form to become known as the "Shakespearean" form.

OVID'S 'METAMORPHOSES'

Oxford's maternal uncle was Arthur Golding, credited with translating Ovid's *Metamorphoses* into the English version of 1567 used by Shakespeare.

SHAKESPEAREAN SONNET

As a young man Oxford wrote the first sonnet of the Elizabethan reign in what would become known much later as the "Shakespearean" form — entitled *Love Thy Choice*, expressing devotion to Queen Elizabeth I

CONSTANT TRUTH

Oxford expressed themes of "constancy" and "truth" in his early sonnet that Shakespeare would express in the same words:

"In constant truth to bide so firm and sure"
(Oxford sonnet to Queen Elizabeth)
"Oaths of thy love, thy truth, thy constancy"
(Sonnet 152 to Queen Elizabeth)

BATH SONNETS

Oxford was with Elizabeth and the Court during her three-day visit in August 1574 to the City of Bath, the only royal visit to Bath of the reign, and this event is reflected in Sonnets 153-154, the epilogue of the sequence.

Oxford shared some basic circumstances with Henry Wriothesley, Third Earl of Southampton, whom most commentators have identified as the younger man or Fair Youth addressed in the long opening series of Sonnets 1-126:

MARRIAGE PROPOSAL: SONNETS 1-17

Oxford in the early 1590's was the prospective father-in-law in negotiations with William Cecil, Lord Burghley for seventeen-year-old Southampton to marry his fifteen-year-old granddaughter Elizabeth Vere (whose birth in 1575 had caused Oxford to deny his paternity and to separate from his marriage to Burghley's daughter Anne Cecil).

Most commentators have perceived Sonnets 1-17 as urging Southampton to accept that marriage proposal.

ROYAL WARDS

Oxford was the first royal ward of Queen Elizabeth, raised in Cecil's custody; Southampton was the eighth and final such "child of state," also raised under Cecil's guardianship.

CECIL PRESSURE

Oxford had been pressured into marrying Burghley's daughter in 1571, entering a Cecil family alliance; and a generation later Southampton was pressured to marry Burghley's granddaughter in 1590-1591, but he refused to enter a Cecil family alliance.

TREASON TRIAL

Oxford sat as highest-ranking earl on the tribunal of peers sitting in judgment of Southampton and Essex at their treason trial.

ACTING & THE STAGE

"As an imperfect actor on the stage"
Sonnet 23

Oxford patronized two acting companies, performed in "interludes" at Court and was well known for his "comedies" or plays.

ALCHEMY

"Gilding pale streams with heavenly alchemy"
Sonnet 33

Oxford studied with astrologer Dr. John Dee, who experimented with alchemy. Both men invested in the Frobisher voyages in search of the Northwest Passage.

ASTRONOMY

"And yet methinks I have astronomy"
Sonnet 14

Oxford was well acquainted with the "astronomy" or astrology practiced by Dr. Dee and was praised for his knowledge of it.

BIBLE

"No, I am that I am..."
Sonnet 121

Oxford wrote to Lord Burghley using the same words in the same tone (the words of God to Moses in the Bible) to protest his spying on him.

CUP
"And to his palate doth prepare the cup"
Sonnet 114
Oxford's ceremonial role as Lord Great Chamberlain included bringing the "tasting cup" to the monarch.

NEW-FANGLED CLOTHES
"Some in their garments, though new-fangled ill"
Sonnet 91
Oxford was the "Italianate Englishman" known (and mocked) for wearing new-fangled clothing from the Continent.

500 YEARS
"O that record could with a backward look,
 Even of five hundred courses of the Sunne"
Sonnet 59
Oxford's earldom extended back five hundred years to the time of William the Conqueror in 1066.

FLOWERS
"Of different flowers in odor and in hue"
Sonnet 98
Oxford was raised amid the great gardens of William Cecil, whose gardener imported flowers never before seen in England -- accounting for Shakespeare's vast botanical knowledge.

FORTY WINTERS
"When forty winters shall besiege thy brow"
Sonnet 2
Oxford was forty in 1590, when most commentators feel the opening sonnets were written.

HAWKS
"Of more delight than hawks or horses be"
Sonnet 91
Oxford was a falconry expert who wrote youthful poetry comparing women to hawks "that fly from man to man."

HIGH BIRTH
"Thy love is better than high birth to me"
Sonnet 91
Oxford was hereditary Lord Great Chamberlain, highest-ranking earl of England by birth.

HORSEMANSHIP
"Then can no horse with my desire keep pace"
Sonnet 51
Oxford was an expert horseback rider and two-time champion of her Majesty's tiltyard.

HOUNDS
"Some in their hawks and hounds"
Sonnet 91
Oxford was steeped from childhood in this favorite pastime of the nobility.

JEWELRY
"As on the finger of a throned Queen,
  The basest Jewel will be well esteemed"
Sonnet 96
Oxford gave the Queen "a fair jewel of gold" with diamonds in 1580.

LAMENESS
"Speak of my lameness, and I straight will halt"
Sonnet 89
Oxford was lamed during a street fight with swords in 1582.

LEGAL KNOWLEDGE
"To guard the lawful reasons on thy part"
Sonnet 49
Oxford studied law at Gray's Inn and served as a judge at the treason trials of Norfolk, Mary Stuart and Essex. His personal letters are filled with evidence of his intimate knowledge of the law.

LUTE
"Mark how one string, sweet husband to another"
Sonnet 8
Oxford was an accomplished musician and wrote music for the lute.

MEDICINE
"Potions of Eisel 'gainst my strong infection"
Sonnet 111
Oxford's surgeon was Dr. George Baker, who dedicated three books to either the earl or his wife Anne Cecil.

MONUMENT"
"And thou in this shalt find thy monument"
Sonnet 107
Oxford wrote to Thomas Bedingfield in 1573 that "I shall erect you such a monument..."

MUSIC
"Music to hear, why hear'st thou music sadly"
Sonnet 8

Oxford was patron of John Farmer, the musical composer, who dedicated two songbooks to him and praised his musical knowledge.

MY NAME
"My name be buried where my body is"
Sonnet 72
Oxford wrote in his early poetry that "the only loss of my good name is of these griefs the ground."

PHYSICAL SKILL
"Some glory in their birth, some in their skill"
Sonnet 91
Oxford challenged all comers in Palermo, Italy to combat with horses and weapons of any kind, but there were no takers.

VIRGINALS
"Upon that blessed wood whose motion sounds"
Sonnet 128
Oxford was an intimate favorite of the Queen, who frequently played on the virginals.

WATER
"Myself bring water for my stain"
Sonnet 109
Oxford was "water-bearer to the monarch" and served as such at the Coronation of King James on July 25, 1603, in his capacity as Lord Great Chamberlain.

WEALTH

"Some glory in their birth, some in their skill,
 Some in their wealth..."
 Sonnet 91

Oxford had inherited great wealth in the form of many estates, but he lost most of this wealth during his lifetime.

Notes

p. 22 – Thomas Thorpe had published works by Christopher Marlowe (posthumous), John Marston and Ben Jonson, among others. Also in 1609 George Eld of Fleet Lane printed *Troilus and Cressida*. William Aspley and John Wright were the two separate booksellers who presumably divided the printed copies of the Sonnets between them for sale and distribution.

p. 23 – "almost certainly a forgery," Katherine Duncan-Jones, editor, *The Arden Shakespeare, Sonnets*, 1997, p. 7; Frank Mathew, *An Image of Shakespeare*, 1922, p. 114; and others suggesting that the Sonnets were suppressed or "stopped" include J.M. Robertson (1926), Hyder Edward Rollins (1944) and Robert Giroux (1982).

p. 23/24 – The 1640 edition, issued by John Benson (and printed by Thomas Cotes) was entitled *Poems: Written by Wil. Shakespeare, Gent*. In the same year Benson published the posthumous poems of Ben Jonson, who had died in 1637. Jonson had played a major role in the First Folio of Shakespeare plays (without any of the poems or sonnets) in 1623; and in my view, the 1640 publication was an extension of the Folio and the effort to obscure the author's identity and to suggest the Stratford man as author. The Benson book of poems and sonnets by "Shakespeare" (and many others) served to obscure the royal story of the Sonnets, a story recording that James of Scotland had stolen the throne of England from the rightful Tudor heir, Henry Earl of Southampton.

p. 24 – The 1711 edition by publisher Bernard Lintott represented the first faithful reprint of a surviving copy of the 1609 quarto. It was placed within a larger volume and advertised, incorrectly, as containing sonnets that "all" had been written "in Praise of his Mistress." It would take several decades more, until 1780, for Edmund Malone to observe that the long opening series (1-126) is addressed to a man; D. Nichol Smith, *Shakespeare's England, Vol. II*, p. 201; Sir George Greenwood, *The Shakespeare Problem Restated*, 1908, p. 83

p. 25 – John Thomas Looney, *"Shakespeare" Identified*, 1920, p. 387; *Love Thy Choice*, Rawlinson Poet MS 85, f. 16, see Chiljan, pp. 197-198

p. 26 – Looney, *Ibid*, pp. 376-380; the entry for Oxford in the Dictionary of National Biography (DNB) was written by Sidney Lee in the late nineteenth century. A newer entry by Alan Nelson (whose 2003 book *Monstrous Adversary* criticizes Oxford's character) is less positive in its point of view and offers less of the evidence that would tend to support his identity as "Shakespeare".

p. 29 – G. Wilson Knight, *The Mutual Flame*, 1962, p. 61; Leslie Hotson, *Mr. W. H.*, 1964, pp. 26-36

p. 30 – Charlton Ogburn, Jr., *The Man Who Was Shakespeare*, 1995, p. 75

p. 33 – "*Rose*" in Sonnet 1 of Q1609 is both capitalized and italicized

p. 35 – W. C. J., *The Athenaeum*, August 20, 1859, p. 250; Charlotte Stopes, *Shakespeare's Sonnets*, 1904, p. xx

p. 43 – The royal progress to Bath (Aug. 21-23, 1574) was Queen Elizabeth's only visit during the reign; see Mary Hill Cole,

The Portable Queen, 1999, p. 187; reacting to Sonnets 153-154, Greenwood writes: "Was Shakespeare at Bath with the Queen? I think it probable that 'Shake-speare' was." – *The Shakespeare Problem Restated*, 1908, p. 127

p. 47 – Roy Strong, *The Cult of Elizabeth*, 1977, p. 14

p. 56 – *Relation made to Sir Francis Englefield by an Englishman named Arthur Dudley, claiming to be the son of Queen Elizabeth* (Madrid, 18th June, 1587), with Englefield's attached letters to Philip of Spain, wherein he recommends to the king that "I am of the opinion that he [Dudley] should not be allowed to get away, but should be kept very secure to prevent his escape," adding that "during this Queen's time they have passed an Act in England, excluding from the succession all but the heirs of the Queen's body." See Frederick Chamberlain, *The Private Character of Queen Elizabeth*, 1922, p. 310

p. 58 – Ogburn, Jr., *The Man Who Was Shakespeare*, 1995

p. 59 – Conyers Read, *Lord Burghley and Queen Elizabeth*, 1960, p. 211

p. 61 – The "goodly boy" borne by the Countess of Southampton on October 6, 1573 would have been conceived nine months earlier in January; but her husband the Second Earl of Southampton was still in the Tower then. He wrote from prison to the Privy Council on February 14, 1573 about "the 16 months close imprisonment" he had suffered to that point – referring to a strict form of confinement that prohibited conjugal visits. (Landsdowne MS 16/23)

p. 61 – "Oxford had argued" with Elizabeth behind closed doors: "The young Earl of Oxford, of that ancient and Very family of the Veres, had a cause or suit that now came before the Queen; which she did not answer so favorably as was expected, checking him, it seems, for his unthriftiness; and hereupon his behavior before her gave her some offense." (Gilbert Talbot, from Greenwich, June 28, 1574, in John Nichol's *Progresses of Elizabeth*)

p. 63 – Oxford "assured Her Majesty that his marriage had not been consummated" – a letter from Dr. Richard Master to Lord Burghley, March 7, 1575, recalling how the Queen had angrily repeated a pledge Oxford had made "openly in the presence chamber of Her Majesty, viz., that if she [his wife Anne] were with child it was not his." (See Alan Nelson, *Monstrous Adversary*, 2003, p. 122)

p. 64 – Thomas Dymocke, etc., see G. P. V. Akrigg, *Shakespeare and The Earl of Southampton*, 1968, pp. 12-14

p. 68 – C. S. Lewis, *English Literature in the Sixteenth Century*, 1954, pp. 503-505; Akrigg, op. cit., p. 206

p. 74 – G. W. Keeton, *Trial for Treason*, 1959, p, 75

p. 75 – Looney, op. cit., pp. 329-332

p. 77 – Hyder Rollins, *A New Variorum Edition of Shakespeare: The Sonnets, Volume II*, 1944, p. 53

p. 83 – Christ in the wilderness: Gospel of Matthew, 4.1-4: "Then was Jesus led up of the Spirit into the wilderness to be tempted of the devil; And when he had fasted forty days and forty nights, he was afterward an hungered; And when the tempter came to him, he said, If thou be the Son of God, command that these stones be made bread; But he answered and said, It is written, Man shall not live by bread alone, but by every word that proceedeth out of the mouth of God." (The latter will be echoed in Sonnet 76: "That every word doth almost tell my name,/ Showing their birth and where they did proceed.")

p. 85 – "where late the sweet birds sang" in Sonnet 73, echoing *The Phoenix and Turtle*, as by "William Shake-speare," 1601, with these dozen concluding lines: "Death is now the Phoenix' nest/ And the Turtle's loyal breast/ To eternity doth rest,/ Leaving no posterity;/ 'Twas not their infirmity,/ It was married chastity./ Truth may seem, but cannot be;/ Beauty brag, but 'tis not she,/ Truth and Beauty buried be./ To this urn let those repair/ That are either true or fair:/ For these dead birds, sigh a prayer."

p. 87 – "a book about scientific visualization…" – *Your Future Self: A Journey to the Frontiers of the New Molecular Medicine*, Thames & Hudson, 1998

p. 90 – Stephen Booth, *Shakespeare's Sonnets*, 1977, p. 202

p. 91 – Booth, op. cit., p. 427; Gerald Massey, *The Secret Drama of Shakespeare's Sonnets Unfolded*, 1866, p. 152

p. 92 – "This is the first of a series of five sonnets…," Duncan-Jones, *Arden Shakespeare, Sonnets*, 1997, p. 164

p.100 – "Princes are 'gods on earth'…" – as in *Pericles*: "Kings are earth's gods," 1.1.103

p. 101-102 – "King James went into a panic…" – Akrigg, pp. 144-145

p. 103 – *A Lover's Complaint* as offering "another angle on the story of Oxford and Elizabeth – the early part, from the vantage point of the Queen herself" – as in this stanza portraying Edward de Vere Lord Oxford as a dazzling, dynamic young man already growing into the great poet-dramatist William Shakespeare:

So on the tip of his subduing tongue
All kinds of arguments and question deep,
All replication prompt and reason strong,
For his advantage still did wake and sleep.
To make the weeper laugh, the laugher weep,
He had the dialect and different skill,
Catching all passions in his craft of will.
A Lover's Complaint, lines 120-126

p. 144 – "a son of mine own" – Oxford was writing to Burghley from Paris on March 17, 1575, upon hearing that his wife was pregnant: "But thereby to take an occasion to return, I am far off from that opinion; for now [as] it hath pleased God to give me a son of mine own (as I hope it is), methinks I have the better occasion to travel…" (Writing in Sonnet 33 of his newly born royal son, he also uses "mine" in that context: "But out alack, he was but one hour mine,/ The region cloud hath masked him from me now.")

Bibliography

THE SONNETS — EDITIONS

Beeching, H. C., *The Sonnets of Shakespeare,* 1904

Booth, Stephen, *Shakespeare's Sonnets,* 1977-2000

Dowden, Edward, *The Sonnets of William Shakespeare,* 1881

Duncan-Jones, Katherine, *Arden Shakespeare's Sonnets,* 1997

Evans, G. Blakemore, *The Sonnets,* 1996

Ingram, W. S., & Redpath, Theodore, *Shakespeare's Sonnets,* 1965

Kerrigan, John, *The Sonnets and A Lover's Complaint,* 1986/1999

Rowse, A. L., *Shakespeare's Sonnets: The Problems Solved,* 1st edition, 1964

Rowse, A. L., *Shakespeare's Sonnets: The Problems Solved,* 2nd edition, 1973

Tucker, T. G., *The Sonnets of Shakespeare,* 1924

Whittemore, Hank, *The Monument,* 2005

Wilson, Dover, *The New Shakespeare: The Sonnets,* 1966

Wright, Louis, *Shakespeare's Sonnets* (Folger), 1967

THE SONNETS — COMMENTARY

Acheson, Arthur, *Mistress Davenant: The Dark Lady of Shakespeare's Sonnets,* 1913

Auden, W. H., *Introduction to Signet Classic, The Sonnets,* 1964

Baldwin, T. W., *On the Literary Genetics of Shakespeare's Poems & Sonnets,* 1950

Dodd, Alfred, *The Mystery of Shake-Speare's Sonnets,* 1947

Fort, J. A., *A Time Scheme for Shakespeare's Sonnets,* 1929

Fowler, Alastair, *Triumphal Forms,* 1970

Frye, Northrop, in *The Riddle of Shakespeare's Sonnets,*

Giroux, Robert, *The Book Known as Q*, 1982

Greenwood, Sir George, *The Shakespeare Problem Restated*, 1908

Hotson, Leslie, *Mr. W. H.*, 1964

Hubler, Edward, *The Sense of Shakespeare's Sonnets*, 1952

Knight, G. Wilson, *The Mutual Flame*, 1962

Knight, G. Wilson, *The Sovereign Flower*, 1958

Lewis, C. S., *English Literature in the Sixteenth Century*, 1954

Malone, Edmund, *Supplement* (to edition of 1778), 1780

Massey, Gerald, *The Secret Drama of Shakespeare's Sonnets Unfolded*, 1866-72

Mathew, Frank, *An Image of Shakespeare*, 1922

Pequigney, Joseph, *Such is My Love: A Study of Shakespeare's Sonnets*, 1985

Rendall, Gerald H., *Personal Clues in Shakespeare Poems & Sonnets*, 1934

Robertson, J.M., *The Problems of the Shakespeare Sonnets*, 1926

Rollins, Hyder Edward, *A New Variorum Edition of Shakespeare: The Sonnets, vol. 2*, 1944

Vendler, Helen, *The Art of Shakespeare's Sonnets*, 1997

Wait, R. J. C., *The Background to Shakespeare's Sonnets*, 1972

Wilson, Dover, *Shakespeare's Sonnets, An Introduction for Historians and Others*, 1963

Wyndham, George, *The Poems of Shakespeare*, 1898

THE SHAKESPEARE PLAYS

The Arden Shakespeare
The Pelican Shakespeare, 2002
The Riverside Shakespeare, 1997

SHAKESPEARE'S WORDS

Crystal, David & Ben, *Shakespeare's Words*, 2002
Oxford English Dictionary (OED)

Schmidt, Alexander, *Shakespeare Lexicon and Quotation Dictionary*, 1902, 1971

SHAKESPEARE COMMENTARY

Bate, Jonathan, *Shakespeare and Ovid*, 1993

Campbell, Lily B., *Shakespeare's Histories: Mirrors of Elizabethan Policy*, 1947/65

Halliday, F. E., *Shakespeare in His Age*, 1956

Knight, G. Wilson, *The Sovereign Flower*, 1958

Wright, Daniel L., *The Anglican Shakespeare*, 1993

SHAKESPEARE REFERENCE

Boyce, Charles, *Shakespeare A to Z*, 1990

Campbell, Oscar James, *Reader's Encyclopedia of Shakespeare*, 1966

Chambers, E. K., *The Elizabethan Stage*, 1923

ELIZABETH I — WRITINGS & SPEECHES

Levine, Joseph M., *Elizabeth I Great Lives Observed*, 1969

Marcus, Leah S., Mueller, Janel, & Rose, Mary Beth, *Elizabeth I Collected Works*, 2000

ELIZABETH I

Camden, William, *Annales*, 1615 & 1625; hypertext edition, Dana F. Sutton

Chamberlain, Frederick, *The Private Character of Queen Elizabeth*, 1920

Cole, Mary Hill, *The Portable Queen: Elizabeth I and the Politics of Ceremony*, 1999

Erickson, Carrolly, *The First Elizabeth*, 1983

Guy, John, ed., *The Reign of Elizabeth I: Court and Culture in the Last Decade*, 1995

Haigh, Christopher, *Elizabeth I: Profiles in Power*, 1988; 1998

Jenkins, Elizabeth, *Elizabeth and Leicester*, 1961

Levin, Carole, *The Heart and Stomach of a King*, 1994

Nichols, John, *Progresses and Public Processions of Queen Elizabeth*, 1823

Shell, Marc, *Elizabeth's Glass*, 1993

Sitwell, Edith, *The Queens and the Hive*, 1962

Strickland, Agnes, *Elizabeth*, 1906

Strong, Roy, *The Cult of Elizabeth*, 1977

Strong, Roy, *Elizabeth R*, 1971

Weir, Alison, *The Life of Elizabeth I*, 1998

Williams, Neville, *The Life and Times of Elizabeth I*, 1972

THE EARL OF SOUTHAMPTON

Akrigg, G. P. V., *Shakespeare and the Earl of Southampton*, 1968

Drake, Nathan, *Shakespeare and His Times*, 1817

Green, Martin, *Wriothesley's Roses*, 1993

Rollet, John, *Was Southampton Regarded as the Son of the Queen*, 1999

Rowse, A. L., *Shakespeare's Southampton*, 1965

Stopes, Charlotte Carmichael, *The Life of Henry, Third Earl of Southampton*, 1922

WILLIAM & ROBERT CECIL

Cecil, Algernon, *A Life of Robert Cecil*, 1915

Cecil, David, *The Cecils of Hatfield House*, 1973

Gordon, Alan, *William Cecil, the Power Behind Elizabeth*, 1935

Read, Conyers, *Mr. Secretary Cecil and Queen Elizabeth*, 1955

Read, Conyers, *Lord Burghley and Queen Elizabeth*, 1960

THE EARL OF ESSEX

Keeton, G. W., *Trial for Treason*, 1959

Lacey, Robert, *Earl of Essex*, 1971

Matter, Joseph Allen, *My Lords and Lady of Essex*, 1969

JAMES I

Akrigg, G. P. V., *Jacobean Pageant: The Court of King James I*, 1962

Akrigg, G. P. V., *Letters of King James VI & I*, 1984

ENGLISH POLITICS, HISTORY, LAW & LIFE

Bellamy, John, *The Tudor Law of Treason*, 1979

Belloc, Hilaire, *A History of England, vol. Iv, 1525-1612*, 1932

Cheney, C. R., *A Handbook of Dates for Students of British History*, 1945/2000

Dictionary of National Biography

Elton, G. R., *The Tudor Constitution*, 1972

Godfrey, Elizabeth, *English Children in the Olden Time, 1907*

Haynes, Alan, *Invisible Power: The Elizabethan Secret Service*, 1992

Harrison, G. B., *An Elizabethan Journal*, 1929

James, Mervyn, *English Politics & the Concept of Honor, Past & Present Society*, 1978

Kempe, Alfred, *Loseley Manuscripts* (Re: 2nd Earl of Southampton), 1836

Levine, Mortimer, *Tudor Dynastic Problems*, 1973

Montgomery, D. H., *The Leading Facts of English History*, 1894

Nicholson, Adam, *God's Secretaries: The Making of the King James Bible*, 2003

Phillips, Graham, & Keatman, Martin, *The Shakespeare Conspiracy*, 1994

Public Record Office, Calendar of Letters and State Papers Relating to English Affairs, 1558-1603, Great Britain, edited by

Martin Hume, 1892-99

Strype, John, *Annals of the Reformation*, 1824

OXFORD'S LETTERS & POEMS

Chiljan, Katherine, *Letters and Poems of Edward, Earl of Oxfor*d, 1998

Fowler, William Plumer, *Shakespeare Revealed in Oxford's Letters*, 1986

May, Steven W., *The Elizabethan Courtier Poets*, 1999

May, Steven W., *The Poems of Edward de Vere, Seventeenth Earl of Oxford and of Robert Devereux, Second Earl of Essex* (Studies in Philology), Early Winter, 1980

OXFORD AUTHORSHIP

Allen, Percy, *The Case for Edward de Vere, 17th Earl of Oxford, as "Shakespeare,"* 1930

Allen, Percy, *The Life Story of Edward de Vere as "William Shakespeare"*, 1932

Anderson, Mark, *Shakespeare By Another Name*, 2005

Beauclerk, Charles, *Shakespeare's Lost Kingdom*, 2010

Caruana, Stephanie, & Sears, Elizabeth, *Oxford's Revenge*, 1989

Clark, Eva Turner, *Hidden Allusions in Shakespeare's Plays*, 1931; Miller ed., 1974

Dickinson, Warren, *The Wonderful Shakespeare Mystery*, 2002

Ford, Gertrude, *A Rose By Any Name*, 1964

Hess, Ron, *The Dark Side of Shakespeare, vols. 1-4*, 2002+

Holmes, Edward, *Discovering Shakespeare*, 2001

Looney, J. T, *"Shakespeare" Identified*, 1920

Miller, Ruth Loyd, *'Shakespeare' Identified & Oxfordian Vistas*, 1975

Nelson, Alan, *Monstrous Adversary*, 2003

Ogburn, Dorothy and Charlton, *The Renaissance Man of England*, 1947

Ogburn, Dorothy and Charlton, *This Star of England*, 1950

Ogburn Jr., Charlton, *The Mysterious William Shakespeare*, 1984, 1992

Ogburn, Jr., Charlton, *The Man Who Was Shakespeare*, 1995

Sears, Elisabeth, *Shakespeare and the Tudor Rose*, 1991; Meadow Geese, 2002

Sobran, Joseph, *Alias Shakespeare*, 1997

Streitz, Paul, *Oxford, Son of Queen Elizabeth I*, 2001

Stritmatter, Roger A., *Edward de Vere's Geneva Bible*, 2001

Ward, B.M., *The Seventeenth Earl of Oxford*, 1928

Whalen, Richard F., *Shakespeare: Who Was He? The Oxford Challenge*, 1994

Index

Sonnet 37: 5, 27, 83
Sonnet 38 (Feb 19, 1601: Trial), 41, 113, 152
Sonnet 39: 5, 26, 83, 142
Sonnet 42: 83, 90, 137, 139, 144, 169, 172, 173, 175
Sonnet 44 (Feb 25, 1601: Essex executed): 113
Sonnet 48: 26
Sonnet 49: 183
Sonnet 51: 181
Sonnet 53: 36
Sonnet 55: 43, 54, 113, 150, 157, 158
Sonnet 56: 144
Sonnet 58: 5, 98, 137, 149
Sonnet 59: 172, 180
Sonnet 60: 5, 152
Sonnet 62: 172
Sonnet 63: 5, 51, 137, 138
Sonnet 64: 51, 144
Sonnet 65: 51
Sonnet 66 (March 19, 1601: reprieve): 31, 83, 85, 114, 115, 147
Sonnets 66-67 (center of the eighty prison sonnets): 116
Sonnet 67: 5, 84, 116
Sonnet 68: 84
Sonnet 70: 5, 84, 98
Sonnet 71: 84
Sonnet 72: 84, 183
Sonnet 73: 84
Sonnet 76: 32, 34, 37, 45, 46, 87, 89, 93, 100, 115, 117, 159
Sonnets 76-77 (Center of Monument): 45, 116
Sonnet 77: 45
Sonnets 78-86 (pen name series a.k.a. "rival" series): 81, 117
Sonnet 80: 85
Sonnet 81: 20, 41, 85, 87, 118, 157, 158

ABOUT THE AUTHOR

Hank Whittemore is author of ten nonfiction books including *The Monument* (2005), for which he received the Excellence in Scholarship Award from the Shakespeare Authorship Studies Centre at Concordia University in Portland OR. In addition to researching in London he performed his one-man show *Shake-speare's Treason,* based on *The Monument,* at Shakespeare's Globe and Cambridge University. He  has delivered papers for the Shakespeare Authorship Studies Conference at Concordia and annual gatherings of the Shakespeare Oxford Society and the Shakespeare Fellowship. His work has appeared in academic journals such as *The Oxfordian, Brief Chronicles* and *Discovering Shakespeare,* a special publication edited by Dr. Daniel Wright. He has won two Emmy awards and the Writers Guild of America Award for documentary television and was a first-place winner of the Little Theatre of Alexandria National One-Act Play Contest. He began his studies of Shakespeare after playing Cassio and Laertes in *Othello* and *Hamlet* at the University of Notre Dame.